MW01677117

KLAUS MOJE

BRUCE GUENTHER ▪ DAN KLEIN

KLAUS MOJE

PORTLAND ART MUSEUM

Published on the occasion of the exhibition, *KLAUS MOJE*, organized by
Bruce Guenther, Portland Art Museum, May 31-September 7, 2008.

The exhibition and publication has been made possible by the generous support of Daniel Greenberg and Susan Steinhauser, Jeffrey and Cynthia Manocherian, Bullseye Glass, the Henry Lea Hillman Jr. Foundation, the Art Alliance for Contemporary Glass, James R. Benson Family, Ann and Mark Edlen, Al Solheim, Dorothy Lemelson, Samuel T. Naito, and Bonnie Serkin and Will Emery. Additional support from the institutional sponsors of the Museum's 2008-2010 Exhibition Series include the James F. and Marion L. Miller Foundation, Bernard B. Kliks Trust, Anne M. Barbey, Pat and Trudy Ritz, Schnitzer Novak Foundation, The Standard, NW Natural, Vibrant Table Catering & Events, and an anonymous donor.

Library of Congress cataloging in progress
ISBN-1-883124-28-X
Published by
Portland Art Museum
1219 SW Park Avenue
Portland, Oregon 97205
www.pam.org

Project manager for Portland Art Museum: Bruce Guenther
Copyedited by John Pierce
Designed by Bryan Potter
Separations by Jerry Sayer
Produced by Bryan Potter Design, Portland, Oregon
Printed and bound by Millcross Litho, Inc, Portland, Oregon

Photography credits:
Photograph © 2007 Museum Associates/LACMA, pgs. 10, 60
The Corning Museum of Glass, Corning, New York, pgs. 32, 35, 50
Toledo Museum of Art, Ohio, p. 33
Photographer Ryan Watson, Portland, Oregon, pgs. 7, 9, 12, 13, 41, 43, 48, 49, 53, 55, 58, 59, 61, 62, 65, 69, 92
Photographer Rob Little, Canberra, Australia, pgs. 11, 15-19, 21, 25, 26, 47, 52, 56, 57, 63, 74, 77-81, 98
Photographer James Dee, New York, pgs. 22-24, 28-31, 36, 37, 39, 40, 42, 45, 51, 54, 64, 66-68, 70, 72, 75, 76
Courtesy of Bullseye Glass Company, pgs. 82, 84-88

Contents

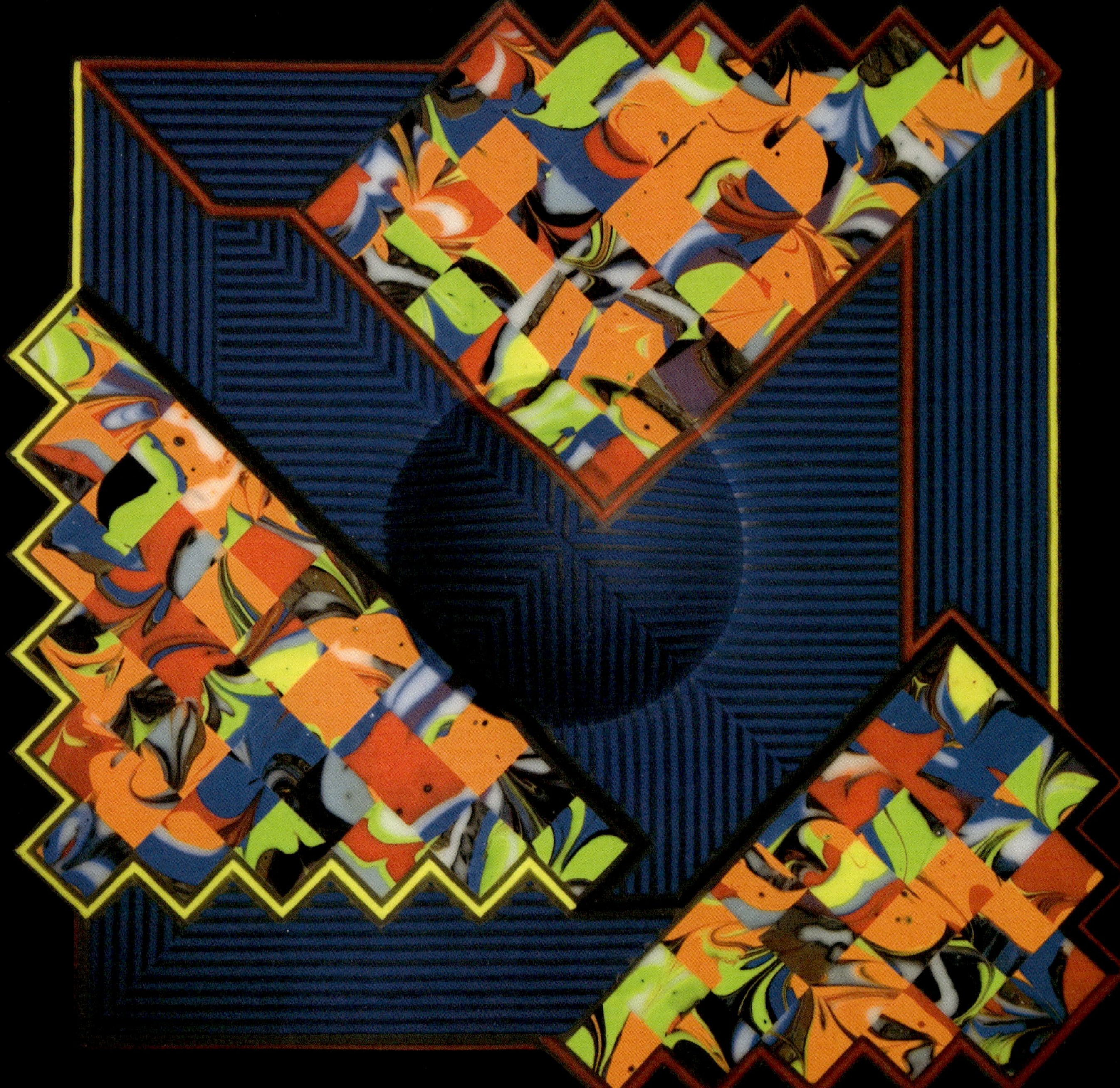

24. Songlines, 1989

Foreword

The Portland Art Museum takes great pleasure in presenting the work of Klaus Moje, one of the most respected artists and teachers working in glass today. Moje's fifty-year commitment to transforming glass-making into a fine art is unparalleled. His career has been marked by an uncompromising dedication to mastering the unique qualities of his chosen medium and embedding it with his creative inspiration. In the end, Moje's sculptural forms are perfectly balanced geometric paintings of glass distinguished by chromatic virtuosity.

Organized by the museum's chief curator, Bruce Guenther, this retrospective review of Moje's art is especially meaningful for the Portland Art Museum, given we share the city with the artist's creative partners, Bullseye Glass and, in particular, its founders Lani McGregor and Dan Schwoerer. Their collaborative journey has produced some of the most important contemporary works of art made of glass. The full cooperation of the artist along with McGregor and Schwoerer at every stage of the exhibition process has made the exhibition and this publication possible. The museum extends its thanks to them and to the many lenders who have parted with their treasured works for the exhibition. We extend our thanks as well to London-based glass specialist, Dan Klein for his thoughtful contributions to this publication.

The museum wishes to acknowledge and thank the lead sponsors for the project Daniel Greenberg and Susan Steinhauser, Jeffrey and Cynthia Manocherian, Bullseye Glass, the Henry Lea Hillman Jr. Foundation, James R. Benson Family, Ann and Mark Edlen, Al Solheim, the Art Alliance for Contemporary Glass, Dorothy Lemelson, Samuel T. Naito, and Bonnie Serkin and Will Emery. Institutional sponsors of the museum's 2008–2010 exhibition series include the James F. and Marion L. Miller Foundation, Bernard B. Kliks Trust, Anne M. Barbey, Pat and Trudy Ritz, Schnitzer Novack Foundation, the Standard, NW Natural, Vibrant Table Catering & Events, and an anonymous donor. The generosity of our supporters is greatly appreciated and is critical to the realization of this stimulating exhibition. ■

Brian J. Ferriso
The Marilyn H. and Dr. Robert B. Pamplin, Jr. Director

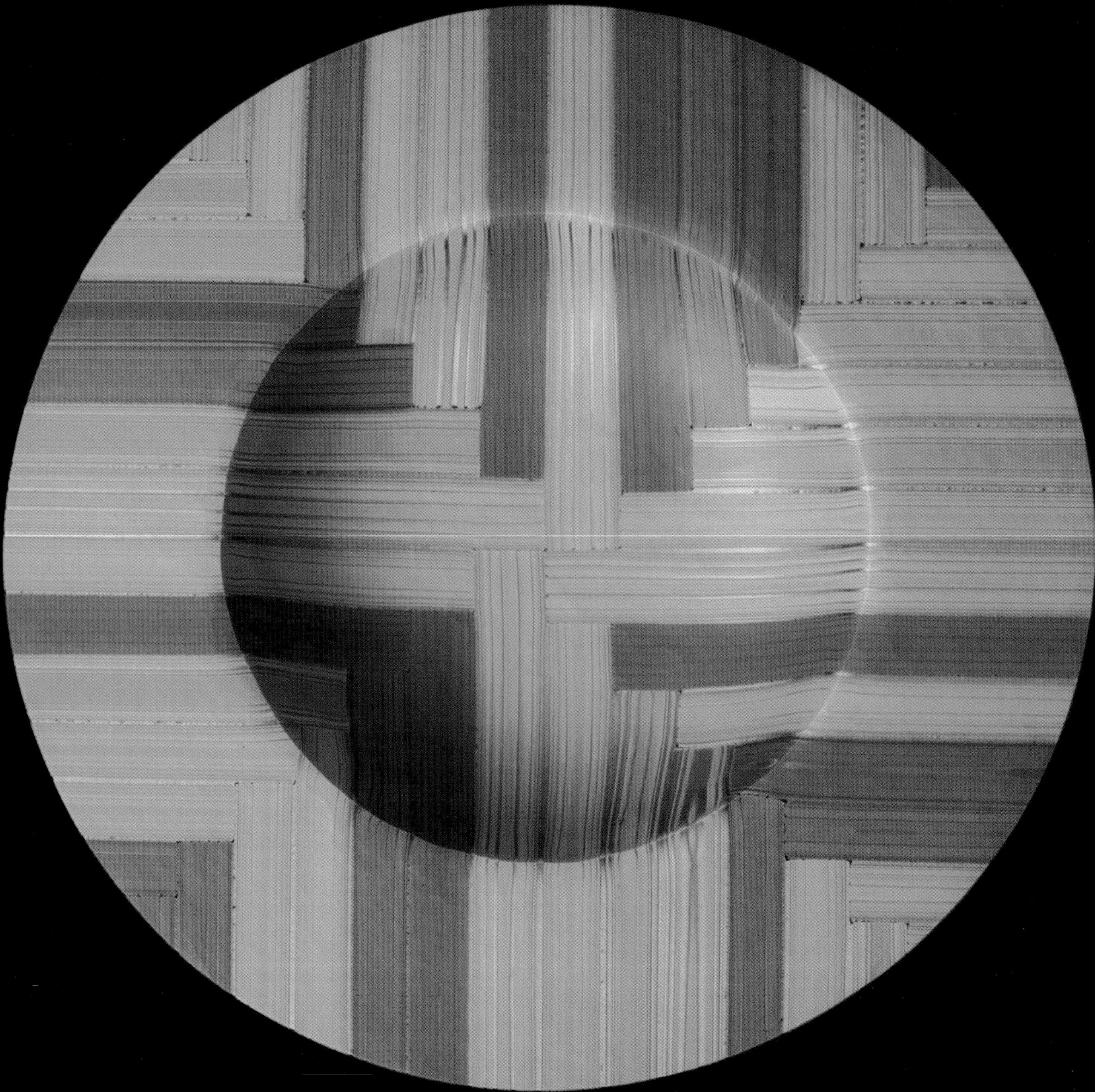

7. Untitled, 1978

A Fused Ground

Bruce Guenther

Participating in the continuing aesthetic dialogue about the art object as autonomous and self-referencing, Klaus Moje has brought innovation and a fresh rigor to the medium of glass through his incorporation of painterly concepts and concerns. Moje, an internationally recognized leader of the fused-glass movement, has pioneered the creation of an art centered in its material and grounded in the historic concepts of geometric abstraction. He has explored over the course of some thirty-five years the terrain of geometry and perception to create artworks that are resolutely optical and outside the structure of narrative and symbols. Moje's work revels in the magic of right angles in a carefully organized, dynamic geometry suffused with the power of undiluted color.

The artist's practice and work is shaped by precedents from the twentieth century. It reverberates with the conceptual concerns of modernist painting, from the compositional tropes of De Stijl and Russian Constructivism to the Bauhaus' codification of design and color principles. Coming to his

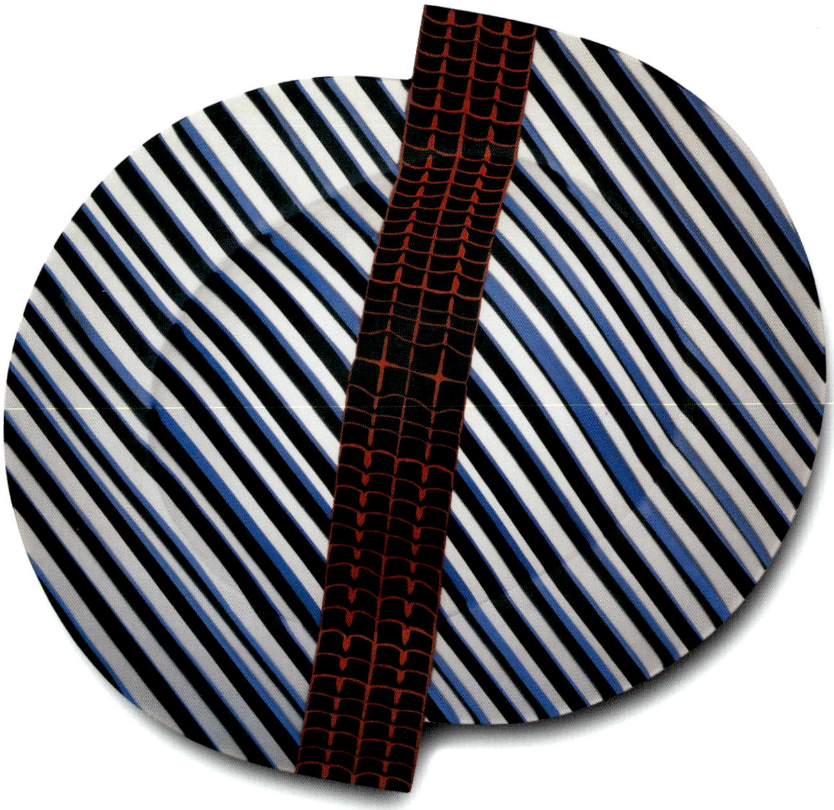

15. Untitled 11, 1983 (#18)

maturity as an artist in post–World War II Europe, Moje was exposed to the continuing influence of the Constructivist aesthetic tradition and more significantly the Bauhaus teachings of Josef Albers (American, born Germany, 1888-1976) and the pure abstraction of Op Art. The basic rules of color and composition as developed in the Bauhaus by Albers and others had become rooted in universities and art schools following the war and shaped the critical dialogue in which Moje participated. Albers's 1963 book *The Interaction of Color* became an instant landmark in the understanding of the function and use of color in painting.

Interestingly, Moje's development as an artist roughly parallels Josef Albers, and he credits him as a major influence on his aesthetic development. Albers was initially trained in a glass technical trade school and, like Moje, first worked with stained glass windows. Hired in 1920 to set up the glass workshop for the Bauhaus, Albers taught glass working, color theory, and design until the school was forced to close under Nazi persecution in 1933. In his glass works, Albers used multilayered sheet glass—opaque, translucent, sandblasted—to create independent geometric panels that were a radical departure for abstract art at the time. The rigorous geometry and systematization of format and process in Albers's works provided a

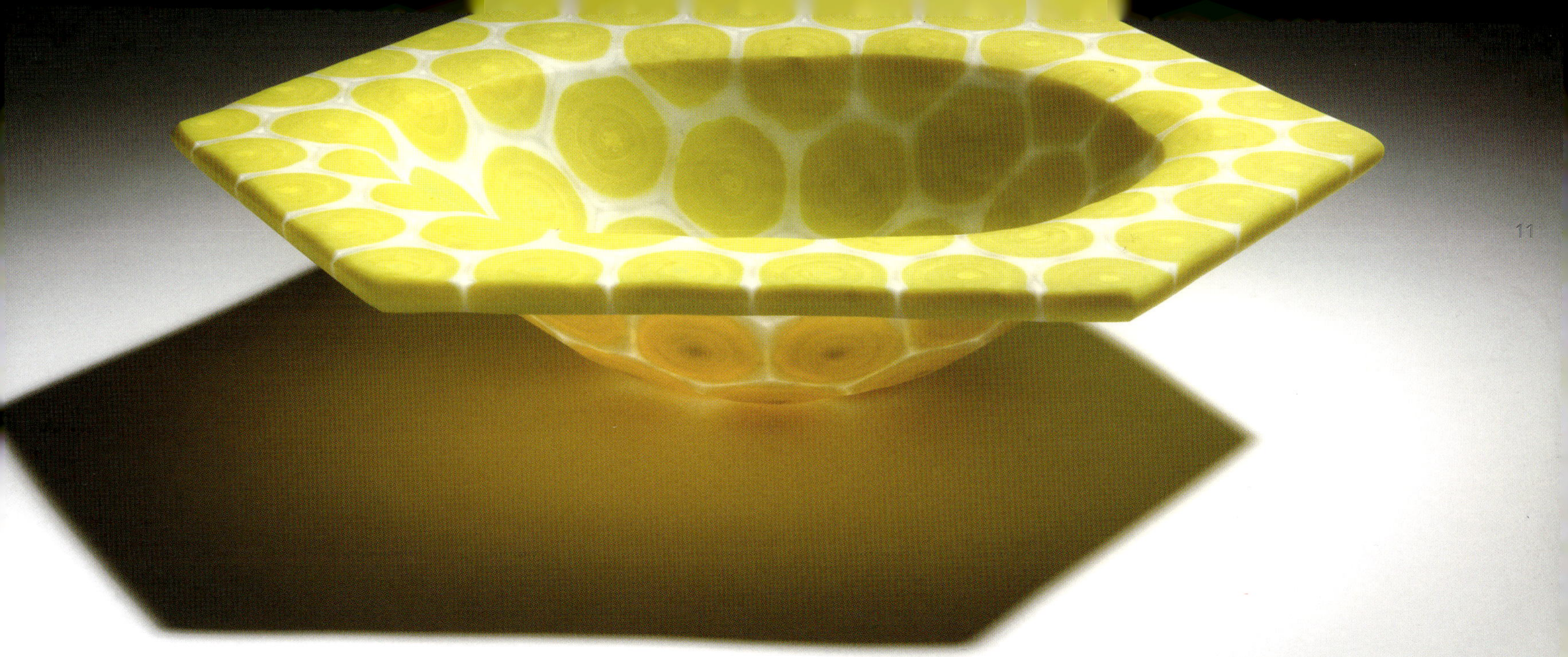

8. Yellow Bowl Oval, 1979

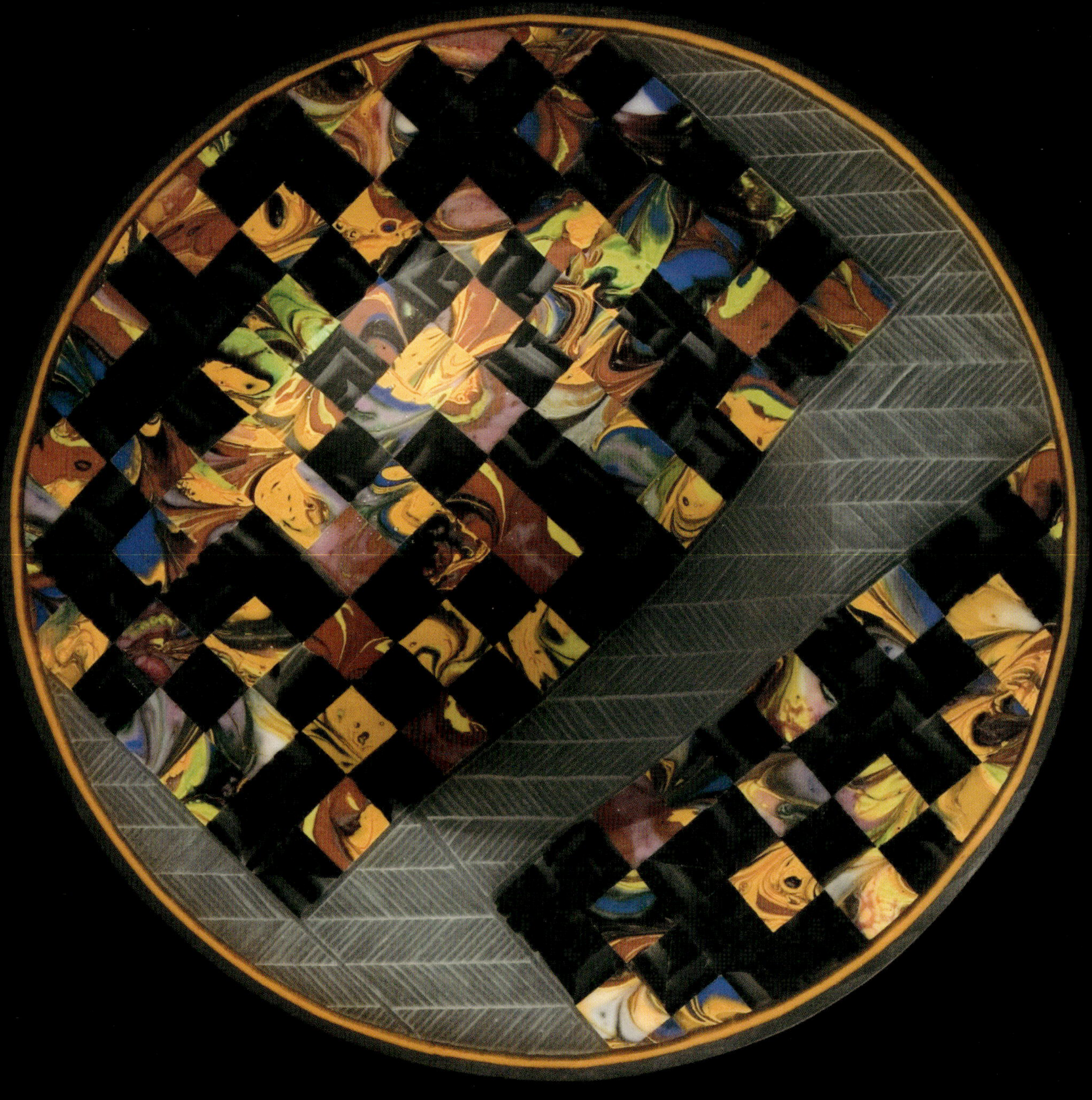

23. Untitled 3, 1989

model for Moje and suggest an historic context for his late multipanel wall works.

The development of Op Art in the 1960s provides another antecedent for understanding the intellectual framework in which Moje's works exist. Positing a nonmetaphorical visual language, Op Art created a mathematically based order of experience that was dominated by the sensory stimulation of color and pattern and depended less on conscious knowledge. Op Art artists saw painting as a system of variables based in geometric color that generated an aesthetic experience outside the socio-cultural domain and centered in the psychophysical. Artists as varied as Victor Vasarely (French, born Hungary, 1906-1997), Bridget Riley (British, born 1931), Richard Anuszkiewicz (American, born 1930), and Yaacov Agam (Israeli, born 1928) pursued a radical re-alignment of the look and experience of a painting by bringing together the science of optics and the graphic oscillations of pattern. The primacy of volition, of the immersive experience, takes center stage in Op painting and changes the way we look, see, and respond to painting. Moje, like many in his generation, picked up the energy and challenge of optical patterning to reinvent the process-bound medium of glass through pattern and color.

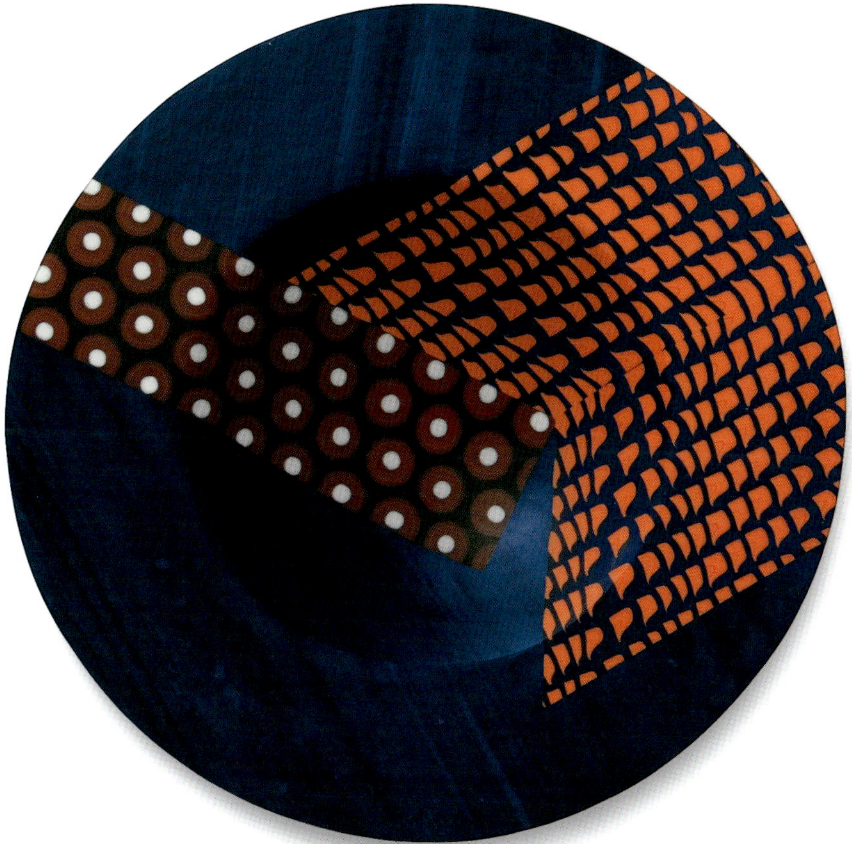

28. Untitled 2, 1990 (#9)

Op Art can be said to have built its aesthetic on mathematical equations and a predictable precision that invites the eyes' rods and cones to fire, challenging perception inside a traditional form. Moje has absorbed its lessons and sense of order and regularity to give his objects a dramatic animation and formal grace. Moje chose early in his production to work with a standardized set of reductive shapes—the circle, the square—that invoke the historic form of a "functional" shallow bowl but assert their reality as an abstraction. Using the schemata of the work, its pattern and color, to establish its relational qualities to history and form. Moje activates the shallow, almost two-dimensional objects spatially by complicating the surface with pattern that moves simultaneously left and right, inward and outward. Using repetition and variation of pattern density and complexity, Moje manipulates the sense of space, light, and motion across the object.

Moje has taken to heart ideas about abstraction like Mondrian's notion of "the living rhythm," achieved by a balance of properly proportioned lines and angles to generate new patterns in glass that inject a quality of movement onto a static object. Using structural variations of pattern to create contiguous or centrifugal compositions, Moje extends or compresses configurations of

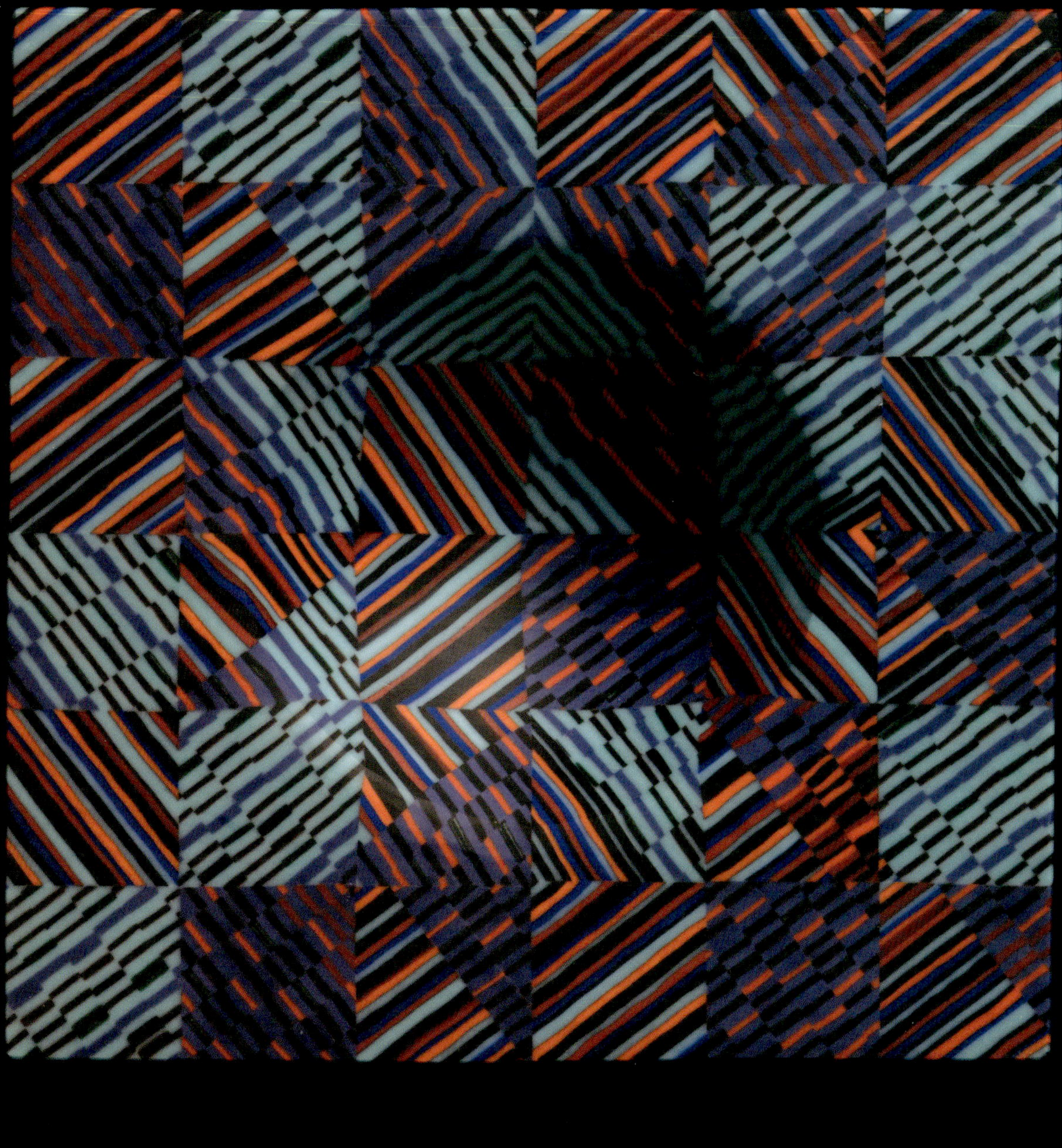

58. Untitled 7, 2006

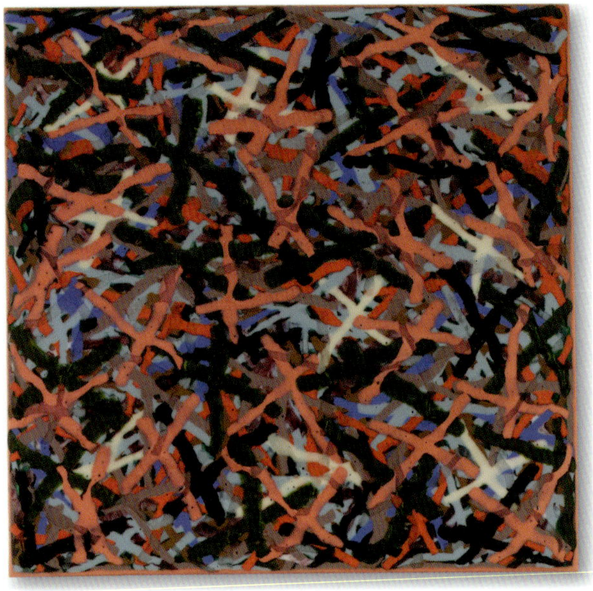

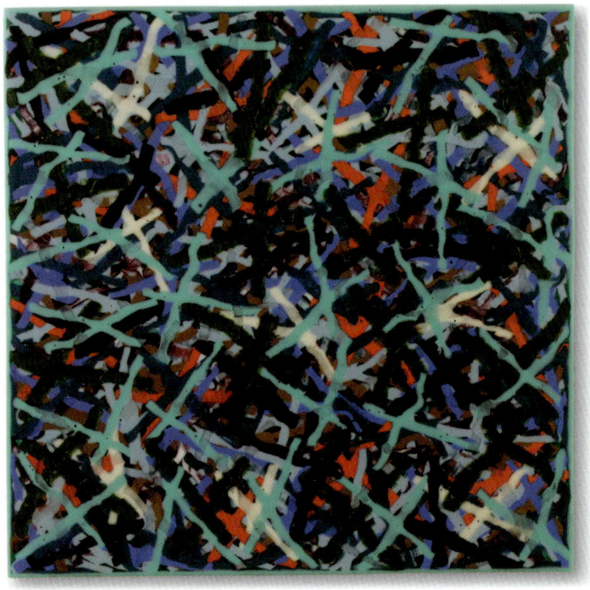

50. Untitled 4, 2005

interlocked shapes. He intentionally creates variables within a continuous pattern as a strategy to generate an optically more unstable structure so that the vessel fluctuates visually, heightening direct visual and visceral experience consciously and unconsciously to alter the brain's function. Moje's complex arrangements of carefully ruled and premeditated shapes break the spatial coherency of the surface but maintain the rigor of their system. Like a work by Agnes Martin (American, born Canada, 1912–2004) in which the painting becomes an exemplifier of its own rulebook, the interplay of pattern in Moje's glass establishes its own rules and rationale within the confines of the material.

The formal armature of the vessel-format and pattern have given Moje the perfect ground for his genius with color. Having absorbed the color theories of Albers and taken his cue from the optical experiments of the late 1960s, Moje exploits the saturation of color and radiant light that is possible with glass to explore the nature of vision both scientific and emotional. Balancing the weighting or dominance of color in the works, Moje plays complementary and contrasting colors against saturation and tint, and transparency against the opacity of the glass to create his works. The process of perception is both a tool

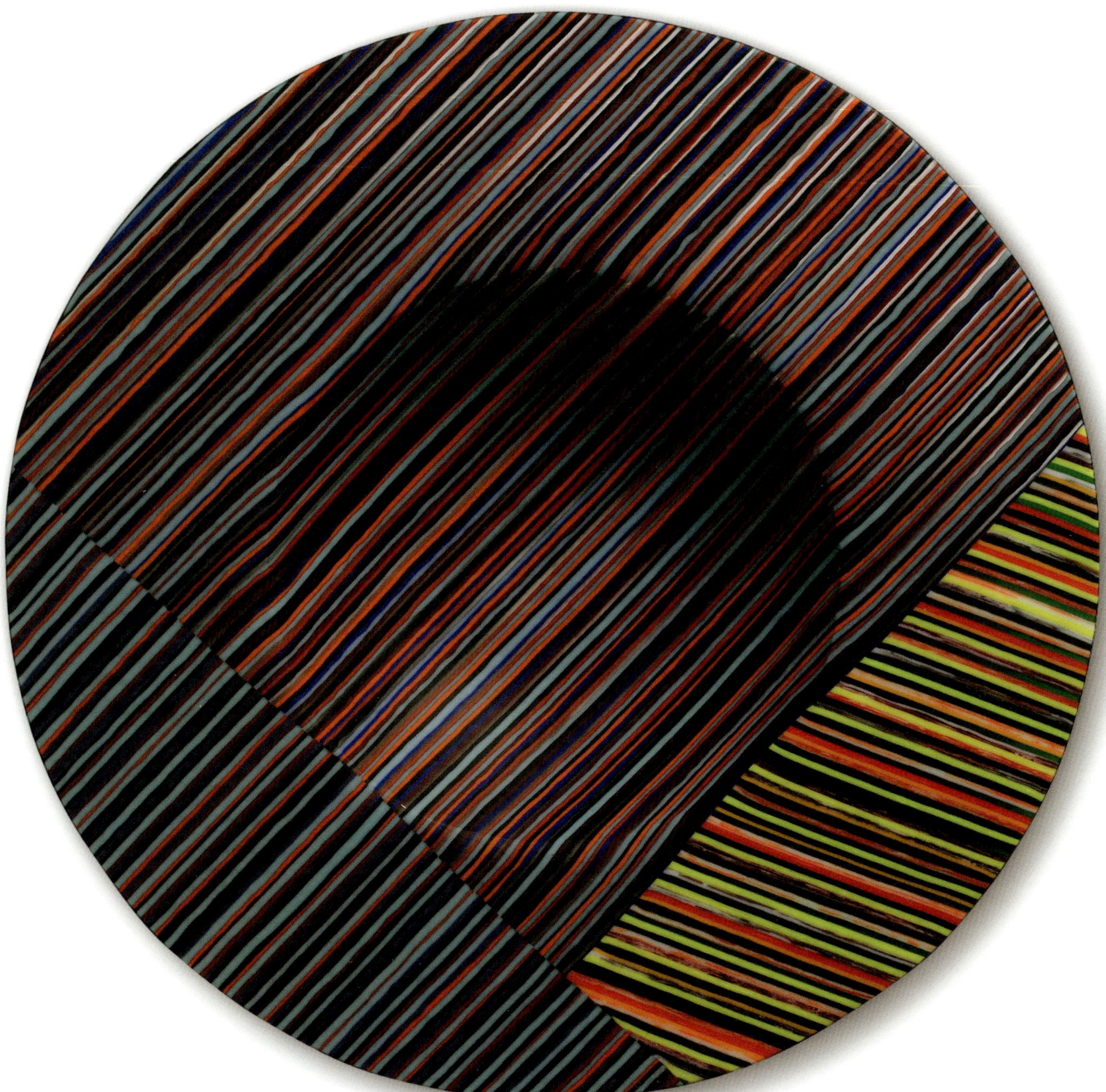

61. Untitled 5, 2006

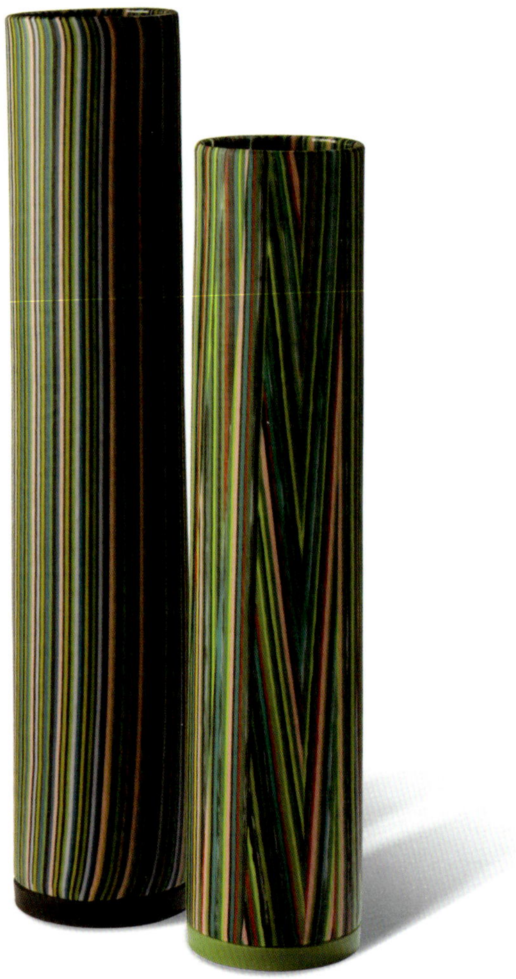

66. Untitled, 2007 (from the *Rolling Lines Series*)

and a subject for the artist as he moves from chromatic harmony to dissonance in successive works. His works calculate the intervals and intensities of the color interactions to create heightened spatial interplays in the patterns, generating retinal vibrations that trigger psychic effect. With each successive body of work over the course of his career, Moje has refined and extended his understanding and use of color so that today there is no effect he cannot achieve with a color and pattern matrix.

The conceptual refinement and formal elegance of Klaus Moje's work is the result in no small part of the physical properties and characteristics of the pieces. The premeditation, patterning, and color choices demand absolute control of the technical production of the works. From the first carved and ground crystal vessels of his youth to the four monumental *Portland Panels*, Moje has understood the object's necessity for an air of singular self-possession. He has become a master at reconciling aesthetic expression with virtuoso technical production to create the objects. From the painstaking assembly of the components to the fusing of the glass through complex and risky grinding and abrading of the surfaces, Moje has mastered the skills to achieve the appropriate translucency and/or opacity of surface to transmit

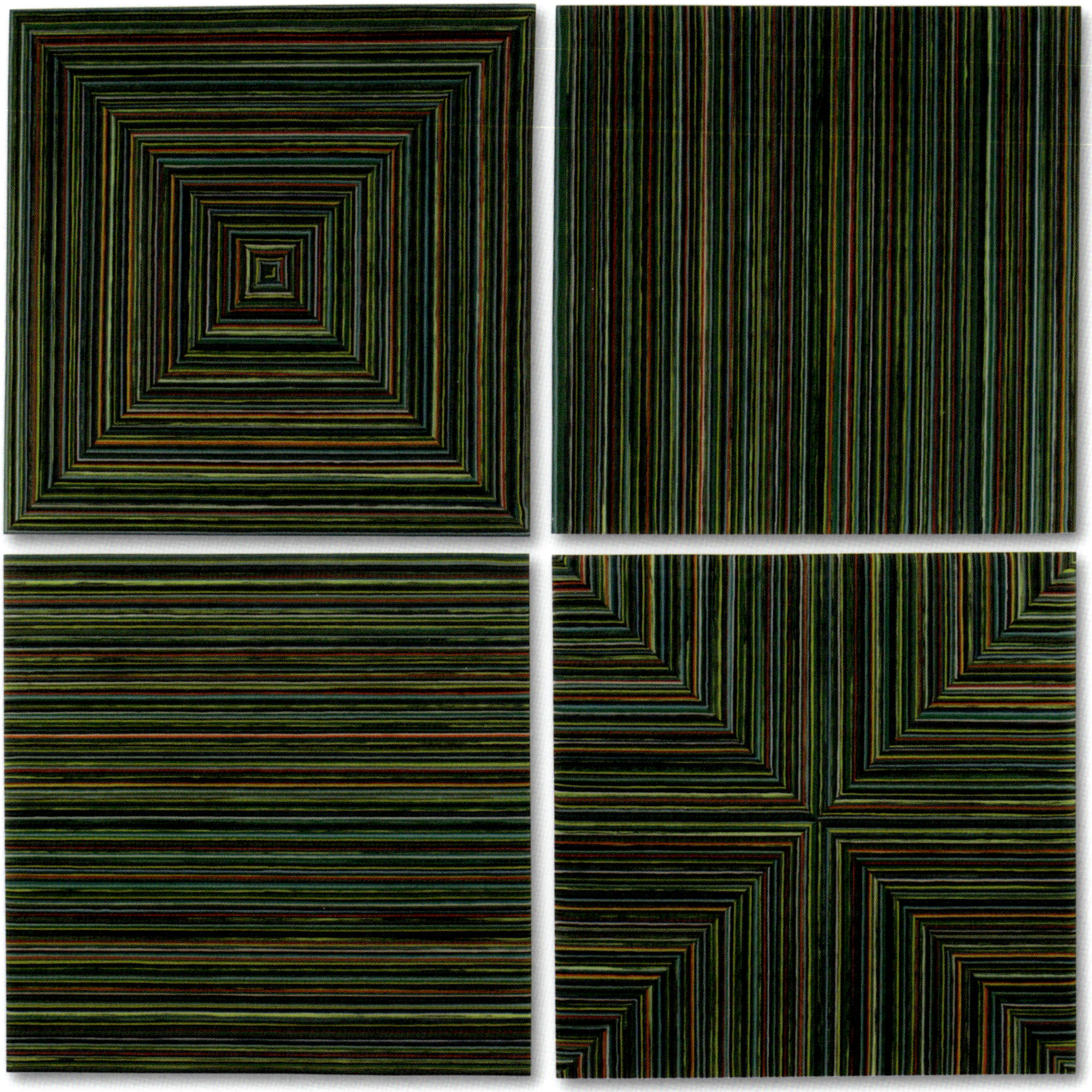

65. Untitled 2, 2006

the right amount of light through the glass, animating the pattern and activating the vibrancy of the color. The purity of Moje's forms with their cleanly honed edges and perfectly machined and ground surfaces speak to his pride in craftsmanship and labor that recalls the pride of a young journeyman glassworker as much as the master artist. The finishing of his works reveals their intrinsic qualities and the visual harmony between complexity of pattern and chromatic saturation, formal invention and schematic character.

Klaus Moje's work is an act of accumulation and faith, system and painterly invention. Valuing structure and order, Moje has invested the power of geometry with the passion of color to create a body of work filled with joy and surprise. Over the course of some thirty-five years, he has quietly brought ideas from the realm of contemporary painting and modern art history into the world of art glass to invigorate and reinvent the medium. Celebrated for his technical innovation and mentoring of young artists, Moje has created a legacy of brilliant works and devoted followers who share his reverence for the clarity of geometric abstraction and saturated color. Both visceral and cerebral, Moje's work unites the polar sensations of order and instability. The viewer experiences equilibrium through oppositions rich in sensuous pleasures and systemic rigor. Without dogma or narrative, Moje gives us the magic of color and the spiritual uplift of light. ■

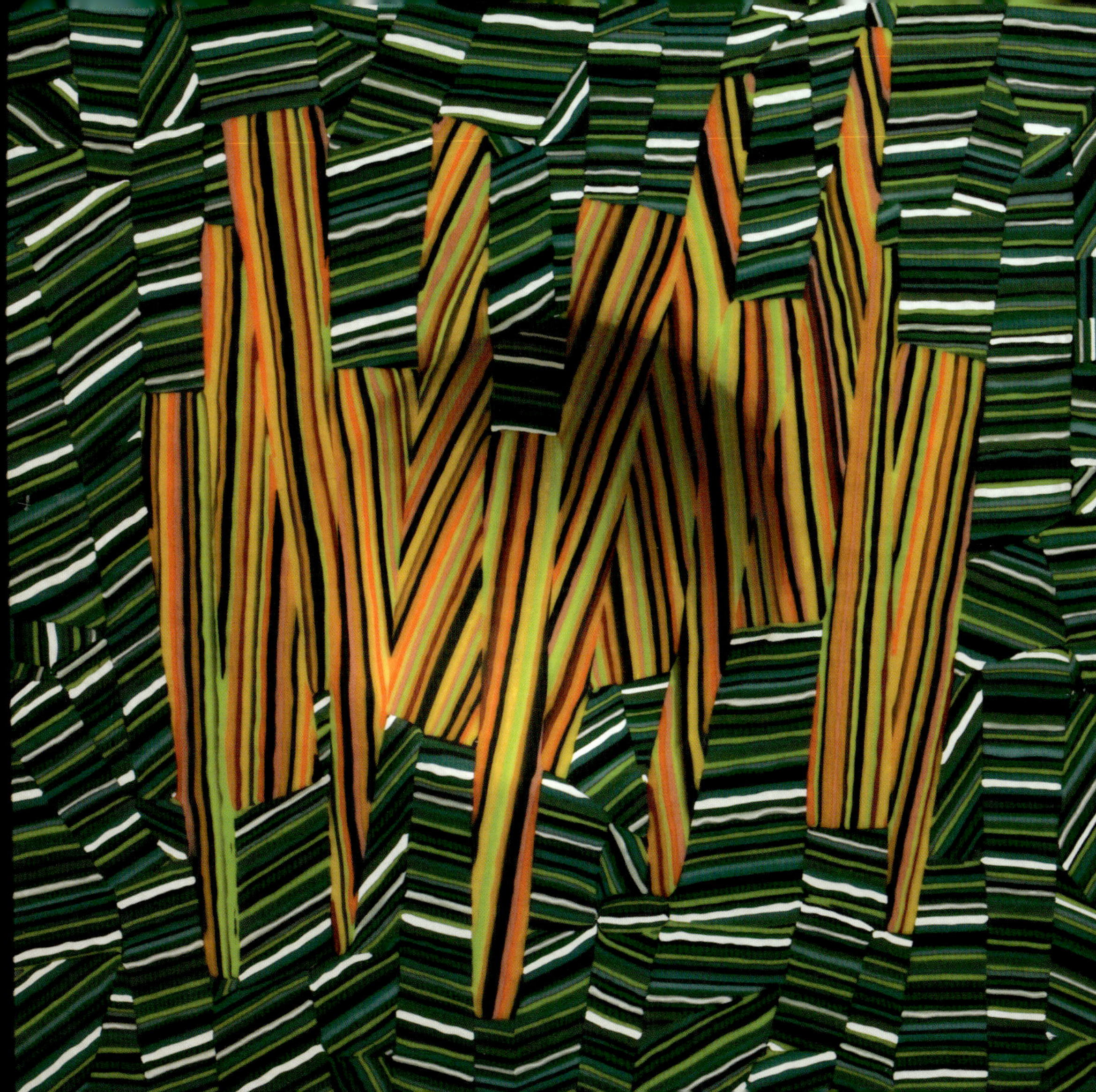

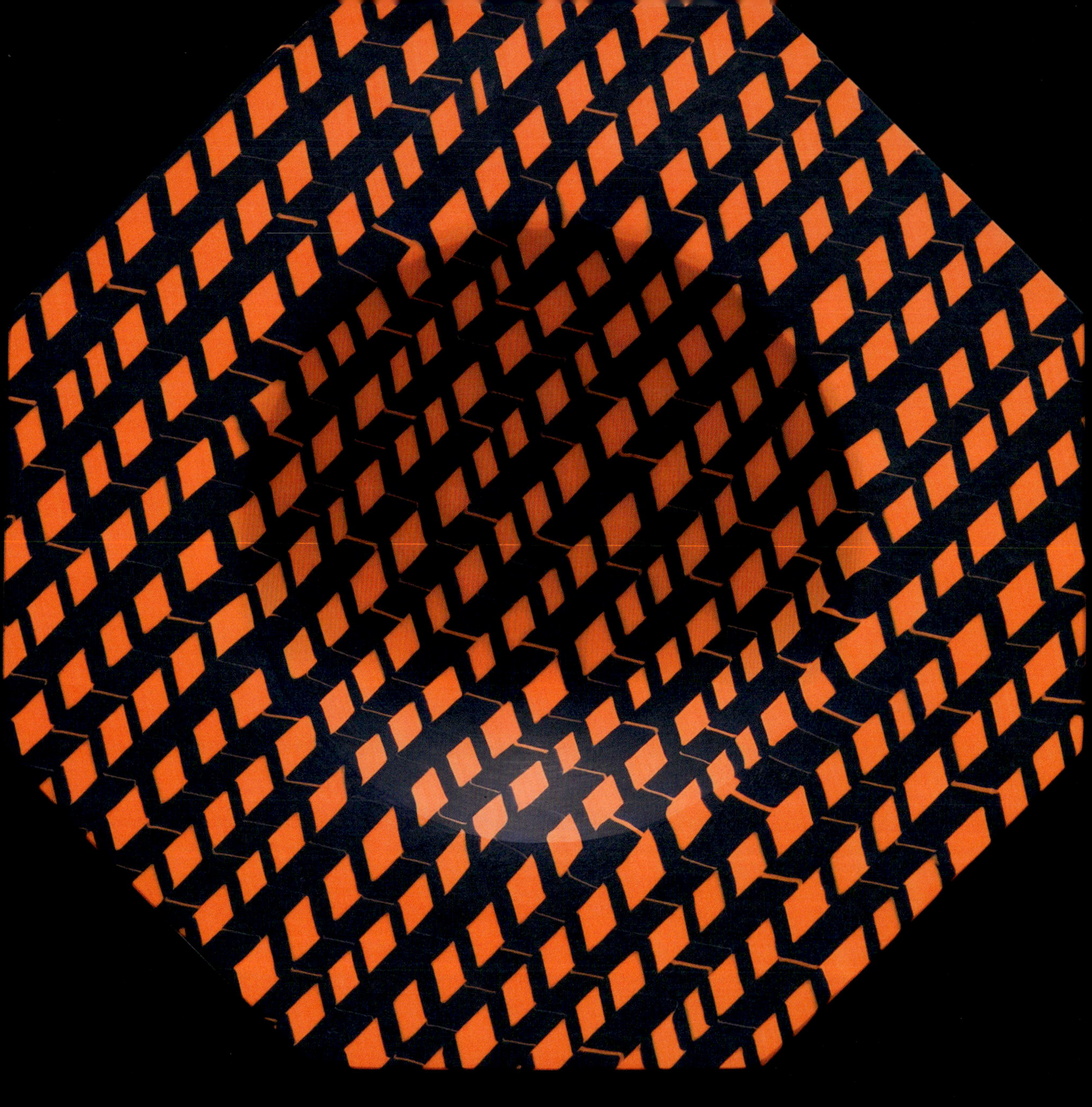

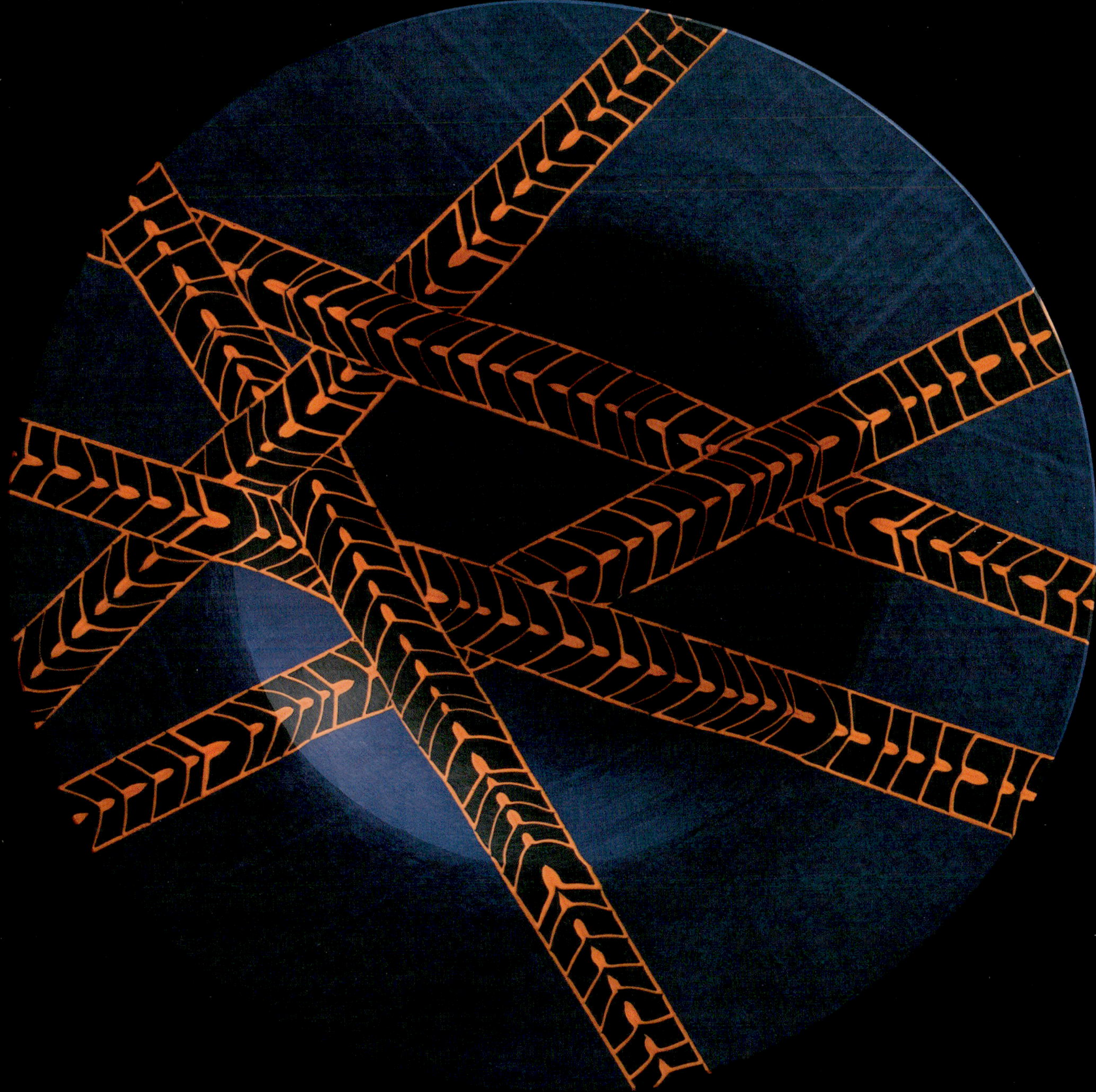

20. Untitled 1, 1986 (#3)

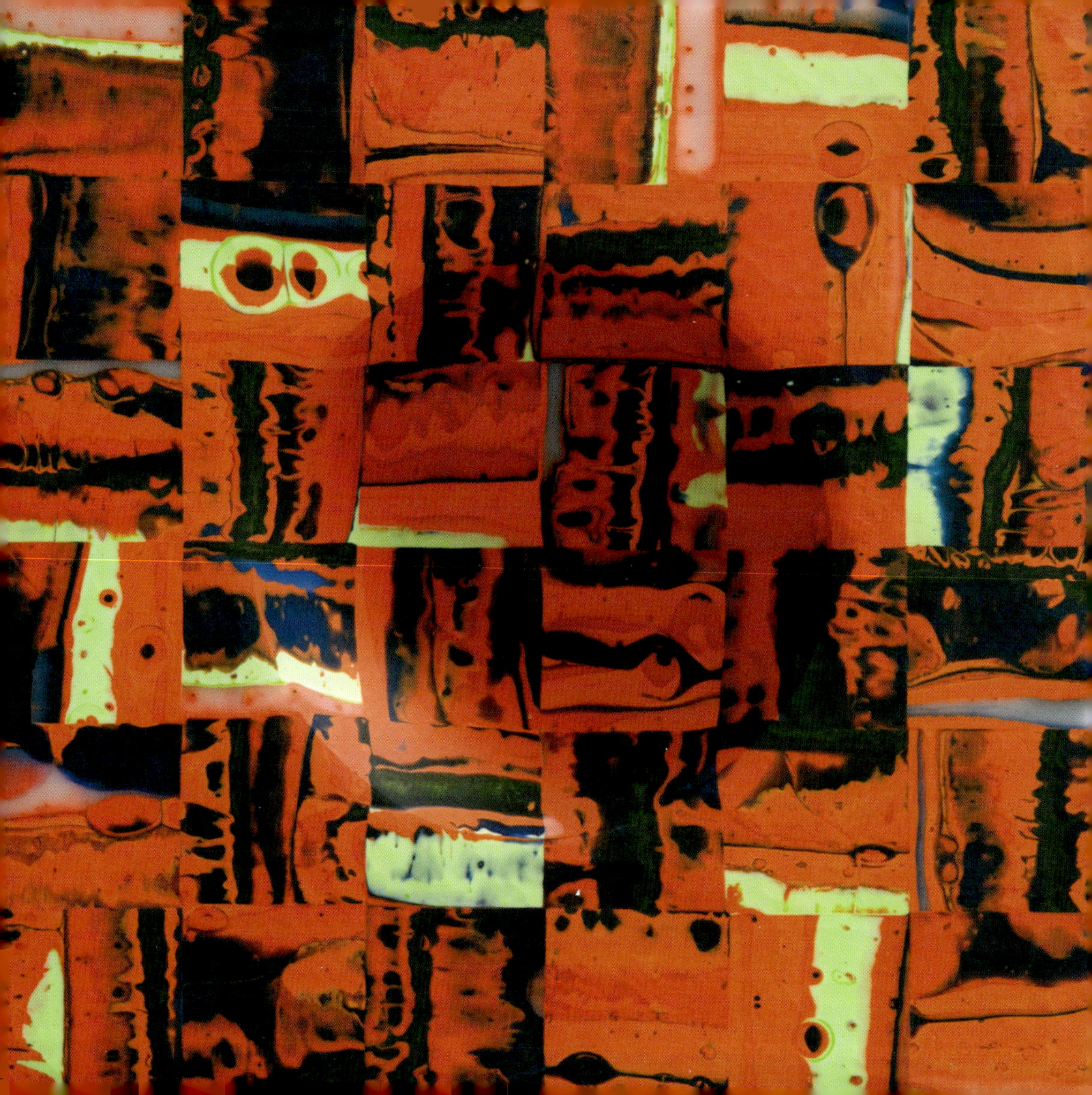

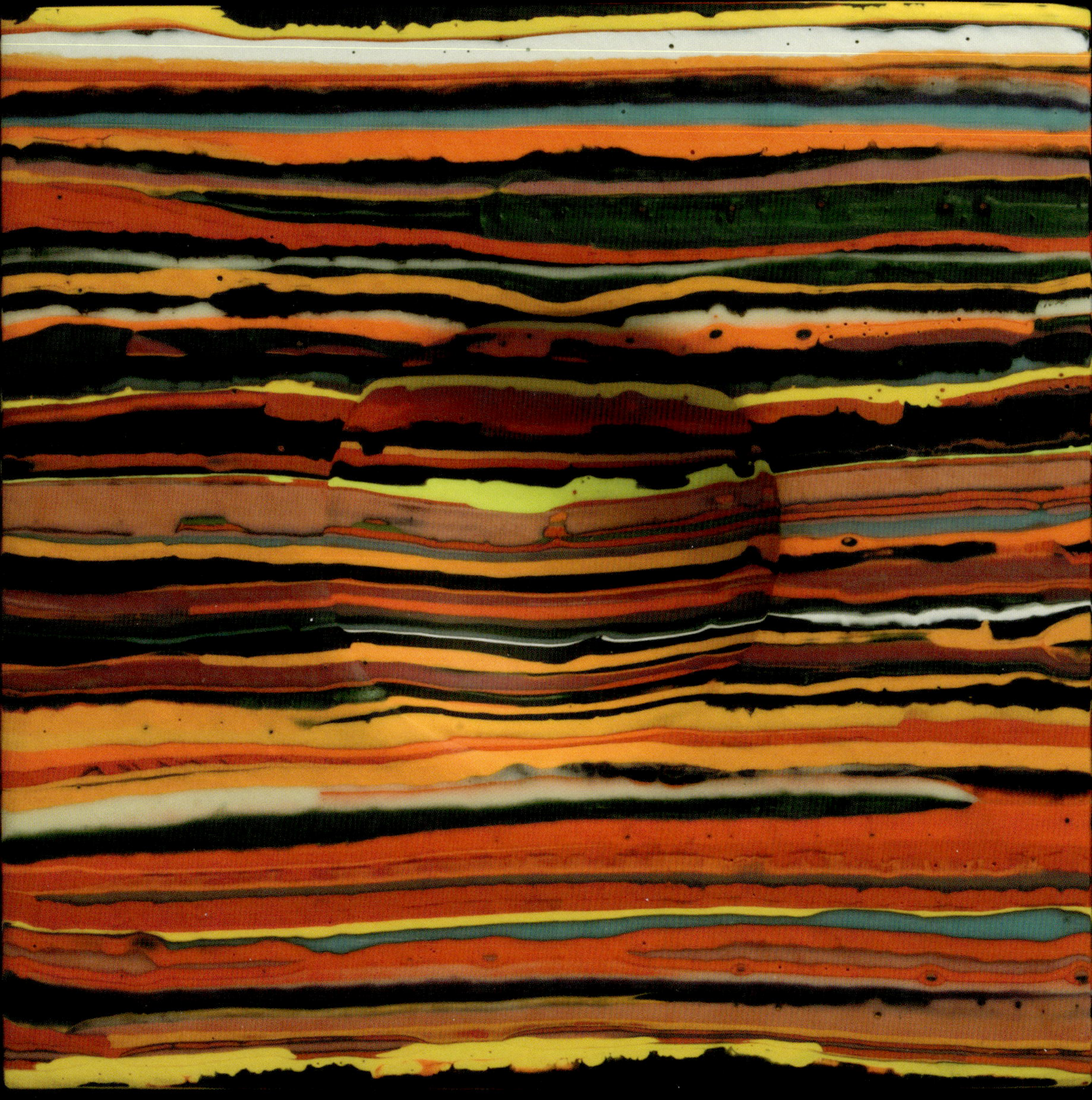

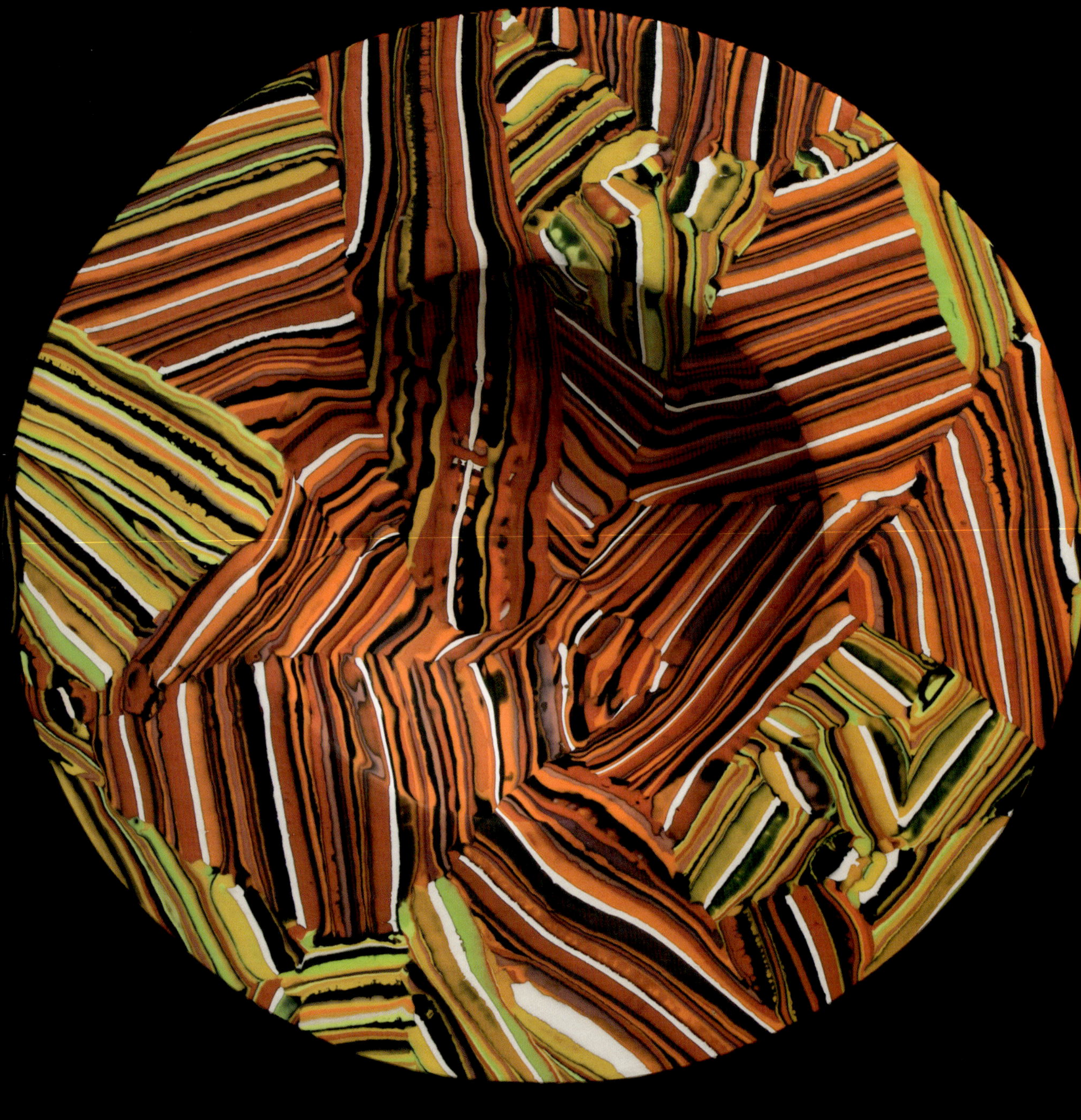

54. Untitled 12, 2006 (from the *Fragment Series*)

Material Understanding and Chromatic Splendor: The Art of Klaus Moje

Dan Klein

In a career that spans nearly fifty years, Klaus Moje has left an indelible mark on the history of glass-making. He makes no bones about loving the material and drawing his inspiration from the magic that it offers. But at the heart of everything he creates lies a passion for color. He uses color as his means of expression, the way a writer uses words.

Color sense is congenital, but the ability to make color communicate requires consummate skill, especially with a material as complex and technically demanding as glass. From the beginning Moje devised his own methods of arranging colors to suit his needs. Nobody taught him to cut, slice, and fuse. Step by step, he invented techniques that would deliver what was in his mind's eye. For although precedents for his way of working date back to the early history of glass, their technical secrets were buried in the past and were certainly not a factor in Moje's innovative approach to creating original

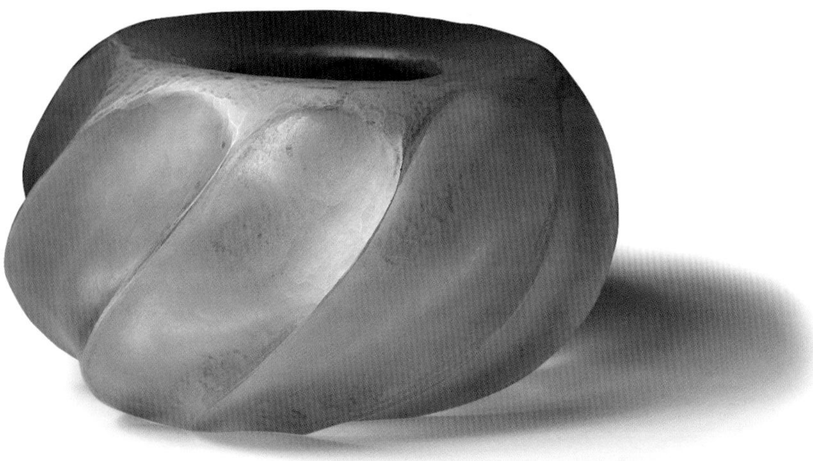

2. Untitled Cut Crystal, late 1970s

works, which combine classical elegance with contemporary aesthetics. His way of making art has turned out to be a classic in its own right, and one that has inspired a generation of glass artists.

Klaus Moje's destiny was decided largely by circumstance and environment as a young adult growing up in post–World War II Hamburg. With the Hugo Moje *Glasschleiferei*, his father's glass-cutting business, glass was already in Moje's background. Added to that were his typically German work ethic, his meditative philosophy as a young Christian, and a burning desire to succeed and "do things well."

Early health setbacks showed Moje's strong will and iron determination. Despite a bout of polio that confined him to a hospital for a year, he became a champion swimmer. His all-around appetite for a full life also included a serious interest in music. Until his mid-thirties he divided his professional life between working in glass and writing songs and lyrics that he performed and recorded. Moje had started a glass-grinding apprenticeship in his father's workshop as a fifteen-year-old, however, and in the end the balance tipped in favor of glass.

Moje's engraving and grinding skills were developed in 1957 at Rheinbach, an industrial glass school, or *Fachschule,* that he attended thanks to a stipend. In 1958–59 he moved to another school at Hadamar. "Both these schools had been established after the war," Moje says, "as teaching institutions which would help rebuild an industry based on hollow ware that had been driven out of Bohemia."[i] Flat glass skills, including painting, lead lighting, sandblasting, and mosaic, were taught at Hadamar, which offered a broader artistic base than the more industrial focus of Rheinbach. Even so, the idea of a career as a glass artist outside the glass industry was not considered an option for someone like Moje, with a *Fachschule* education.

One of the most significant episodes of Moje's early professional life was a request in 1960 to work on a window designed by Lothar Schreyer for the Apostel Kirche in Lurup, Hamburg. This was an important commission, which also marked the beginning of a working partnership between Moje and his first wife, Isgard Moje Wohlgemuth. *The Meditation Window*, a series of thirteen panels based on the Holy Trinity, was a patchwork of brilliant prismatic color effects with a three-dimensional feel, the result of multiple overlays with carving and deep etching.

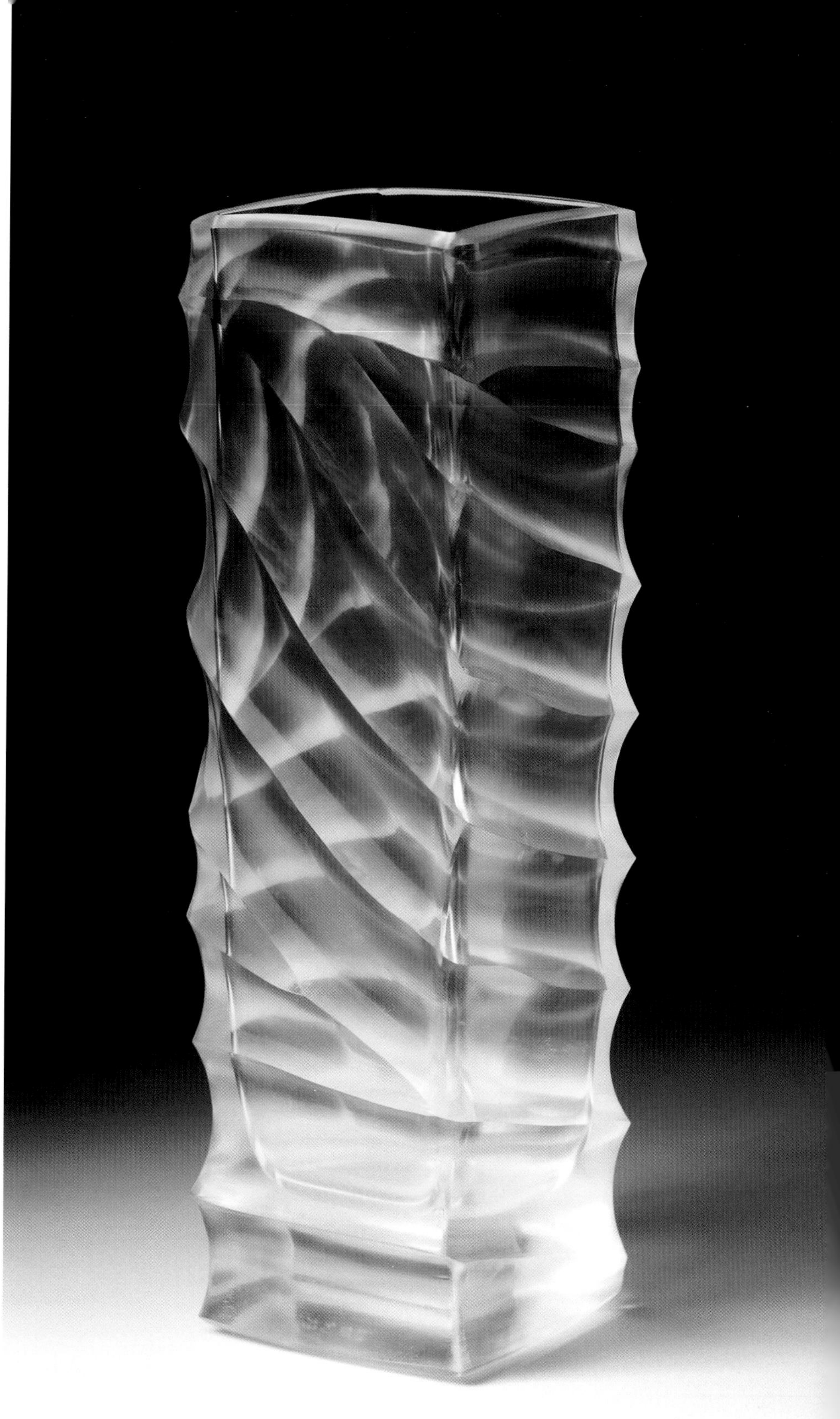

3. Untitled Cut Crystal, late 1970s

Lothar Schreyer had trained as a lawyer, exhibited expressionist paintings, and been a leading light in Hamburg's avant-garde theater. He was appointed by Walter Gropius to run the Bauhaus Theater Workshop in 1921. Moje recalls, "This work brought me in touch with a wide range of people who had studied at the Bauhaus, people who had the same attitude to materials as myself." Some aspects of Bauhaus teaching went against the grain with Moje, but it is clear that he was influenced by the Bauhaus manifesto's claims that there should be "no essential difference between the artist and the craftsman" and that "the artist is an exalted craftsman."[ii]

Thanks to the initiative of another *Bauhaüsler*, the renowned designer and metalsmith Wolfgang Tümpl, Klaus and Isgard Moje received their first invitation to exhibit work in a museum, at a juried annual Christmas fair at the Museum für Kunst und Gewerbe in Hamburg. In 1982, a mutual respect for Bauhaus ethics must have helped when Udo Sellbach, a noted Australian printmaker and teacher, invited Moje to teach at the Canberra School of Art. In Canberra Moje established the renowned Glass Workshop, where it became clear that his work ethic, respect for craftsmanship, and range of expression as a colorist reflected aspects of

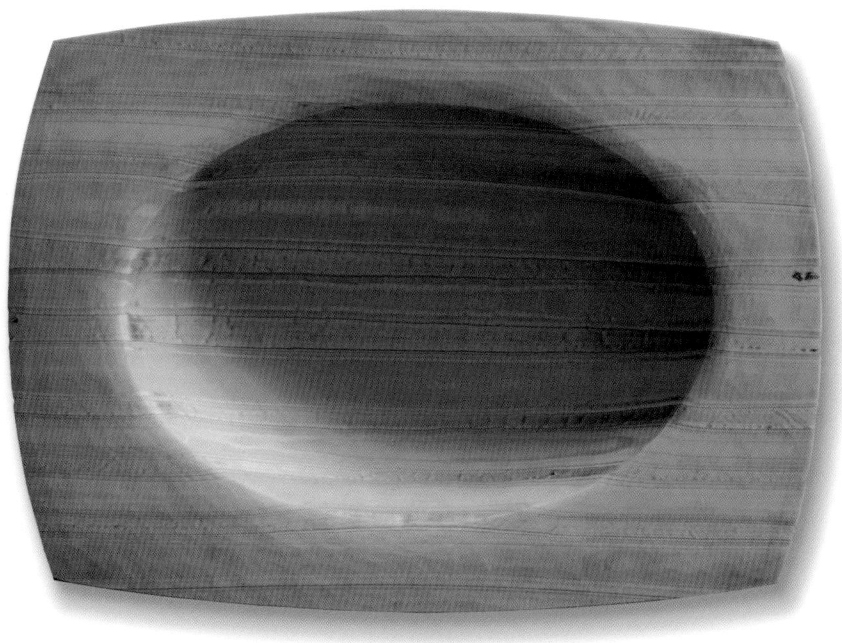

11. Untitled, 1981

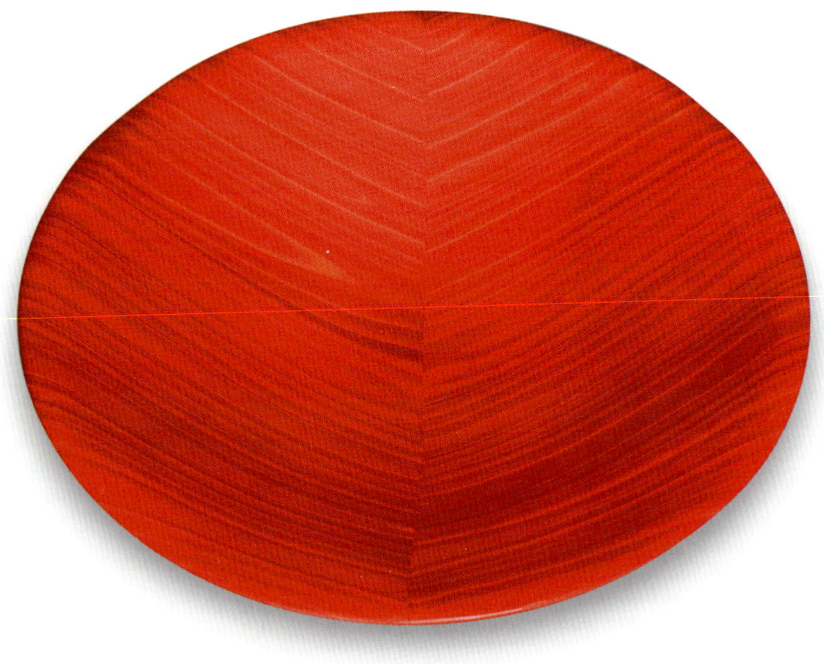

5. Mosaic Glass Bowl, 1977

Bauhaus teaching. "It never entered my mind that I would teach Bauhaus style," says Moje, "but the Bauhaus aesthetic is embedded in me...What I brought with me was to teach *truth to materials* and the experience of the materials that you need to make exceptional work."

Even before the Bauhaus connection, however, Moje had the deepest respect for skill and perfect finish. At the outset of his career he had made carved and engraved pieces in the manner of German predecessors such as Wilhelm von Eiff, whose training had been similar to Moje's and who for Moje was "the first person I ever saw as a master figure in glass." Moje's early pieces demonstrated his talent for using tradition as the key to self-expression, but he also had the ability to think outside conventions, which led him to make his first mosaic pieces.

The first mosaic pieces that he felt comfortable about exhibiting date from the mid-1970s. By that time he had ironed out some basic technical issues, which allowed him to control what he was doing. "I knew nothing when I made my first piece of mosaic...I just cut up the sausage and learned by trial and error...In my early years I used to say that there was twenty percent of the good Lord in my pieces."

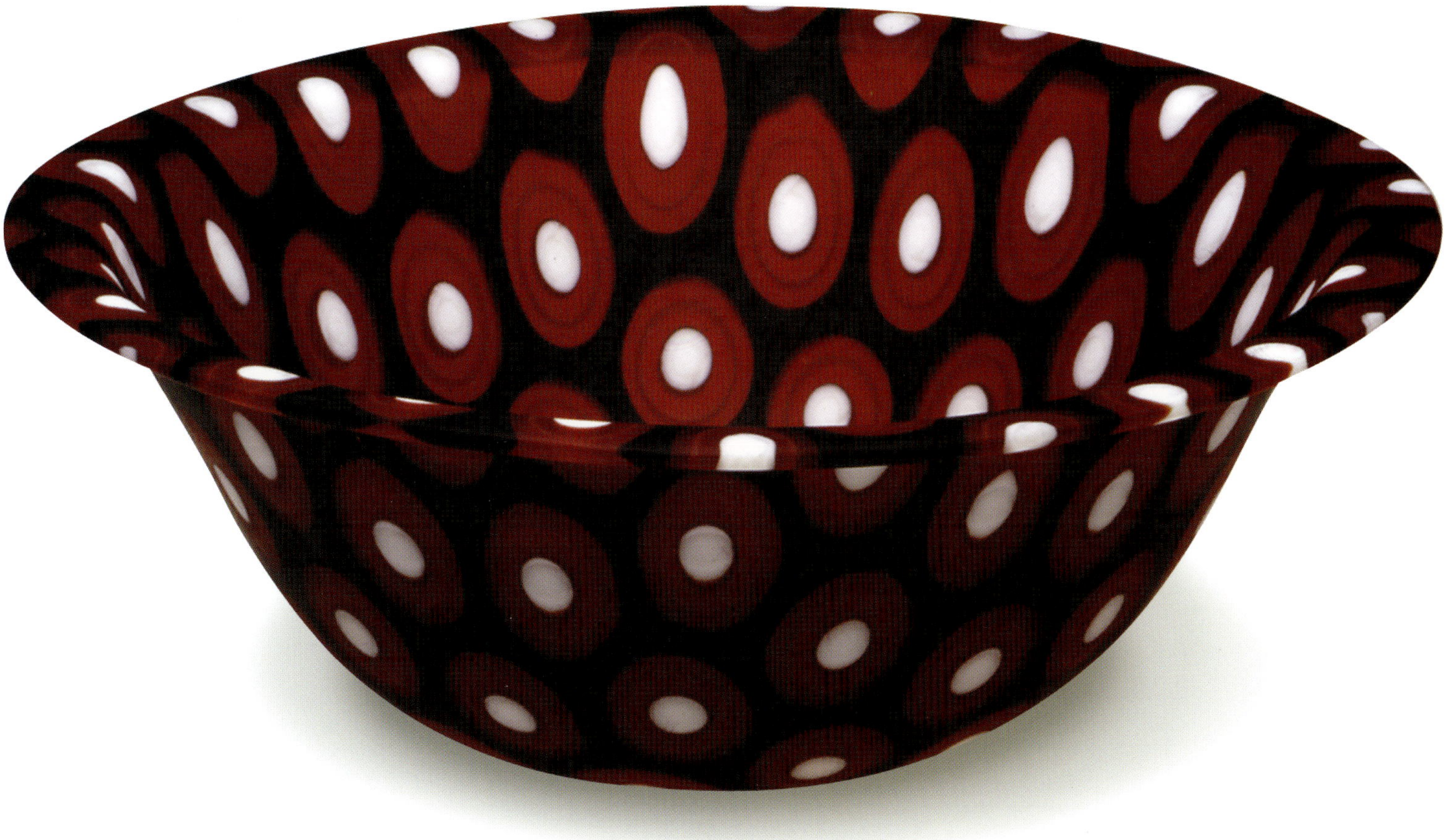

9. Untitled Bowl (Lifesaver), 1979

"The first piece that came out was an all-white mosaic bowl," says Moje. "Lucky as I was, I showed it in an exhibition, and the director of the Hamburg Museum [Axel von Saldern] saw the bowl and praised it. I thought 'My God I have something there!' Having made that first piece and having that praise was important. If I had not had it, I wouldn't have continued. I didn't know anything about annealing, or color compatibility. I just worked." His method of working was to cut, assemble, fuse, slump, grind, and polish—a process that in essence has remained the same throughout his career.

By this time Moje was known in the glass world nationally and internationally, mainly as a prominent artist. But he had also played an active ambassadorial role in the glass community, representing Germany at the World Craft Council meetings from 1969 on. A gallery he opened in Hamburg in 1973, in partnership with Isgard Moje, had also increased his visibility. The pioneering gallery, perhaps the first in Europe or anywhere to be devoted to the contemporary art of glass, exhibited the work of young artists from around the world, including Erwin Eisch, Ann Wärff/Wolff, Dale Chihuly, and William Morris. "We started the gallery because there was no support system available," says Moje.

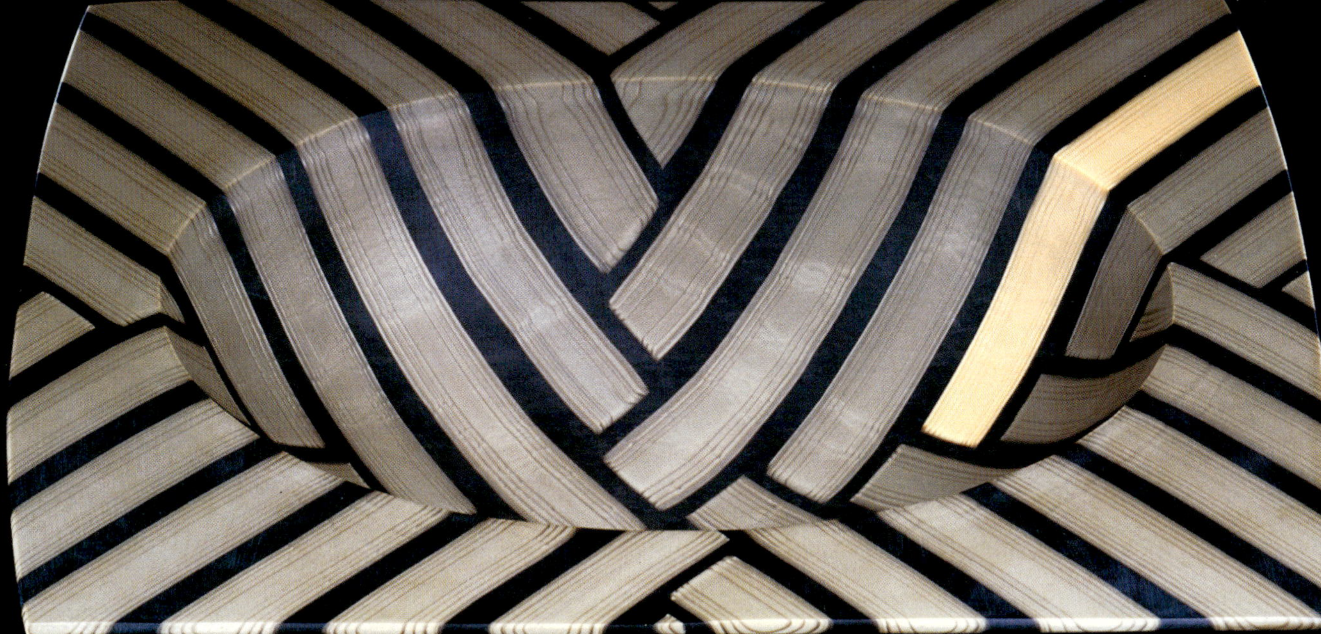

10. Untitled, 1980

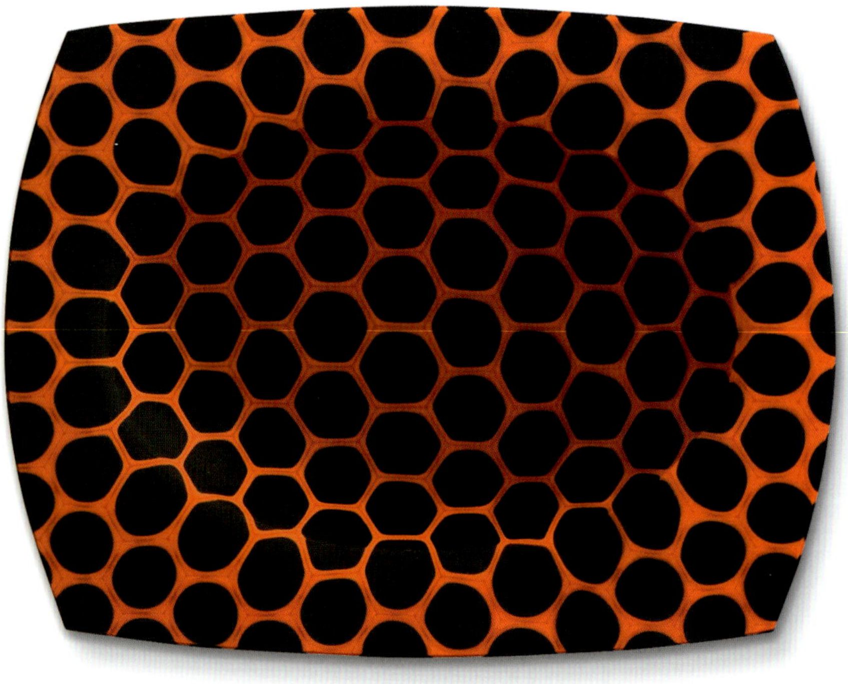

13. Untitled, c. 1982

The success of the gallery inspired others to open theirs (for instance, Edith Gottschalk and Galerie SM in Frankfurt) and encouraged other artists to believe in studio glass as a career.

In his studio Moje continued to experiment and developed an infatuation with colored glass. For Moje, brought up in the German tradition of treating glass more like a hard stone than a ductile fluid, the possibilities of color had been limited. Now colored glass unlocked a passion for polychromy. "My desire for color came early, but I was not able to realize it technically," says Moje. "Isgard used paint [on glass], but the intensity of it was not enough for me."

He had learned about color balance from the Lothar Schreyer project and seen how Schreyer proportioned and blended color. He had also admired Egyptian glass on a visit to the Corning Museum of Glass in 1972. But the way Moje came to work with color was groundbreaking, not only for him but for the art of contemporary glass generally. No other glass artist was investigating the possibilities of color fusing at that time.

On a routine buying trip for materials he noticed the colored glass rods (used principally for

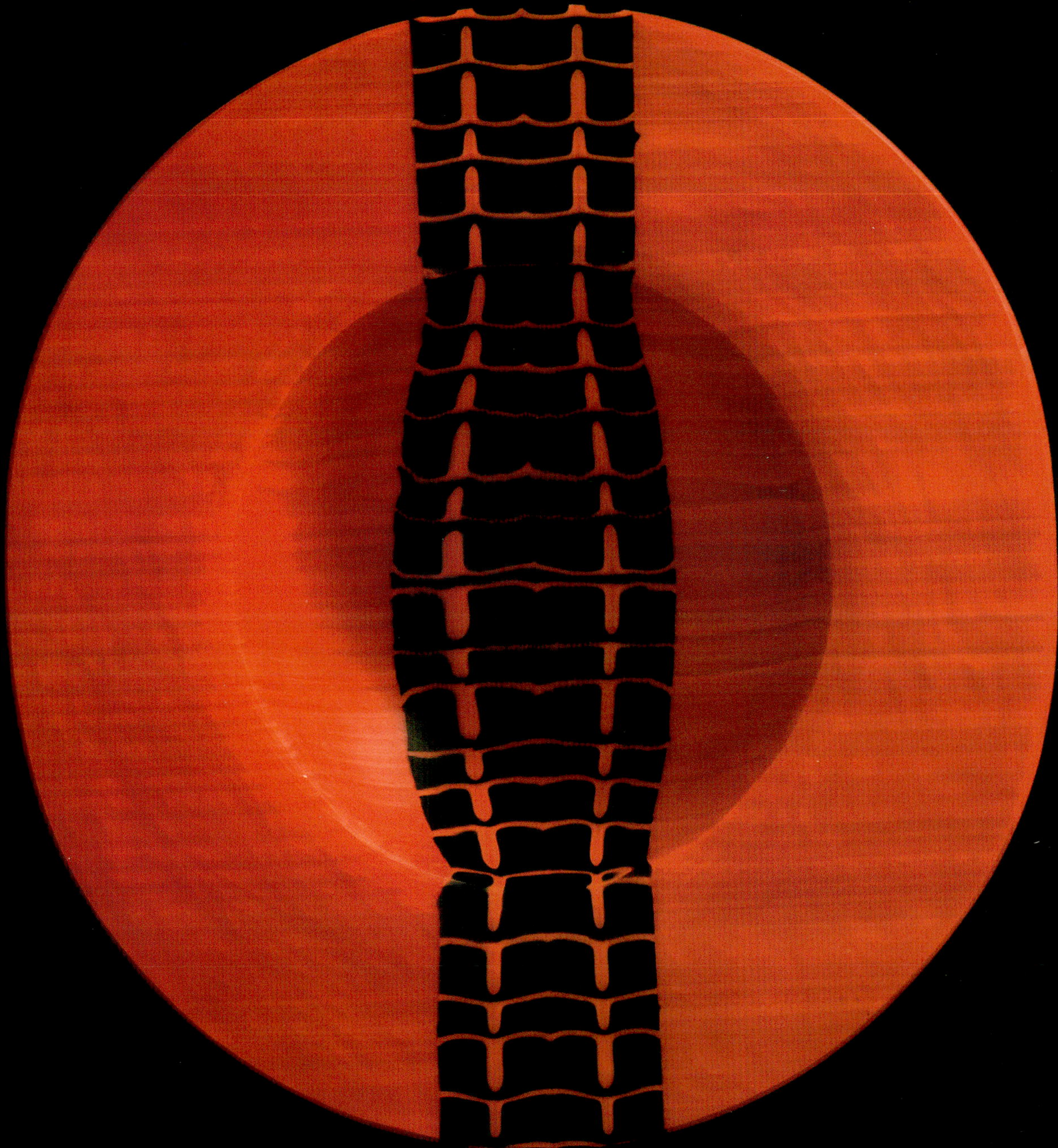

14. Untitled 5, 1982

jewellery, buttons, and chandeliers) at the German manufacturer Hessenglaswerke. It was a eureka moment. He began using the rods in his mosaics work. The circular and oval forms of these early mosaic pieces were simple and traditional, but their modernist geometric decoration, composed of colored lines, circles, and squares, raised them to another plane. His work stood out because of its unmistakable authorship, its distinctive visual language, and its lively color palette, seen only in blown glass at that time. The sheen of opaque color on Moje's fused glass created a much different aesthetic from that generated by the transparent palette of hot glass, as different as watercolors from paints.

In 1979, at the invitation of Dale Chihuly, Moje made his first trip to Pilchuck Glass School near Seattle as a guest lecturer and course leader. The "American way of thinking" broadened his horizons, even if there was guarded appreciation for what he had to offer. His audience of American and international students and glassmakers was intrigued by his unfamiliar way of working because the emphasis at the time was on hot-glass processes. This same year Lino Tagliapietra, the famed Venetian glassblower, also made his first visit to Pilchuck.

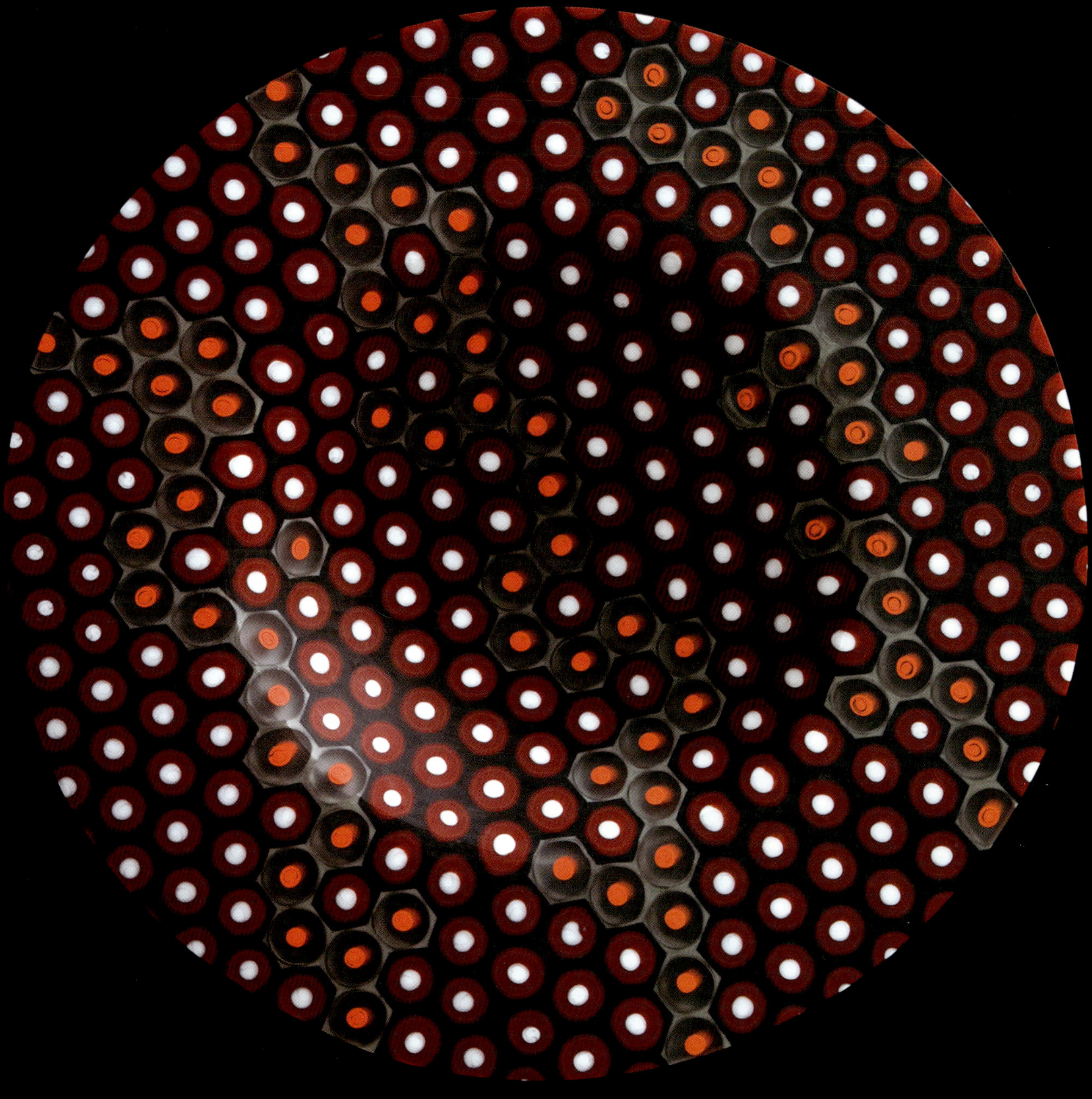

18. Untitled, 1986

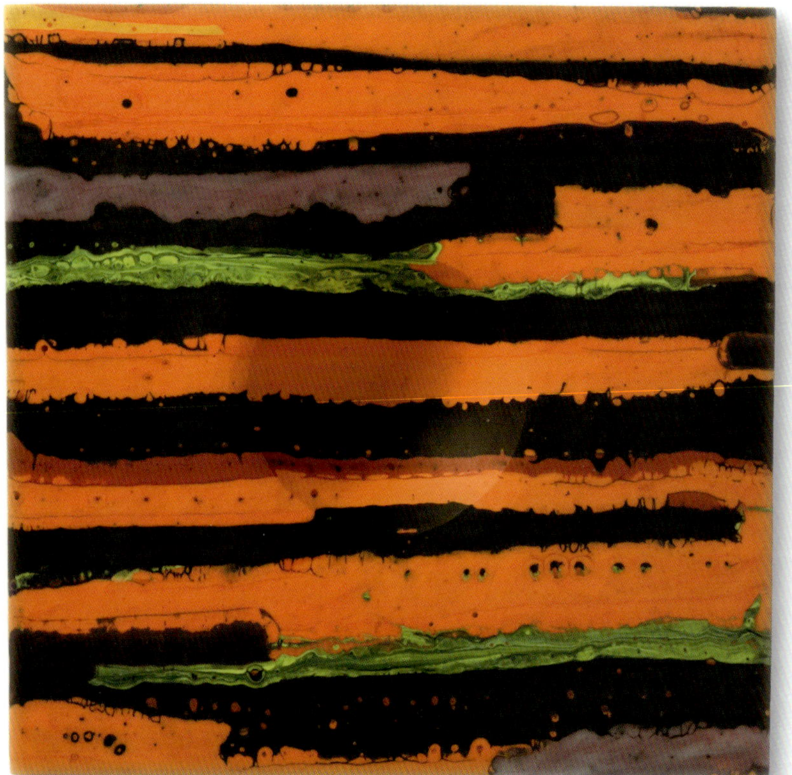

36. Untitled 4, 1994 (#34)

Moje remembers, "The Italians were looking at the Scandinavians, the Scandinavians at the Italians, the Americans were in awe of both of them, and I was watching all of them together. There was hardly any equipment available, not even a functional kiln. I don't even know what we called fusing then; we had no definition for it. What I did was certainly not seen as art."

Marvin Lipofsky, who in 1967 founded the glass program at the California College of Arts and Crafts, was among Moje's Pilchuck audience and invited him to teach in California. Lipofsky had the foresight to tell his students, "You may see something you will not appreciate at the moment, but watch this guy."[iii]

Moje had certainly left an impression, if no inkling of the developments yet to come. These developments might never have materialized if one of his students at Pilchuck, Boyce Lundstrom, had not invited him to visit Bullseye Glass Company in Portland, where Lundstrom and his partner, Dan Schwoerer, were researching the possibilities of producing glass specifically for glass fusing. Upon meeting with Moje at Bullseye, Lundstrom and Schwoerer made a promise, saying, "We want to develop this glass for you." Two years later, says Moje, "A box of glass landed on my doorstep in Hamburg."

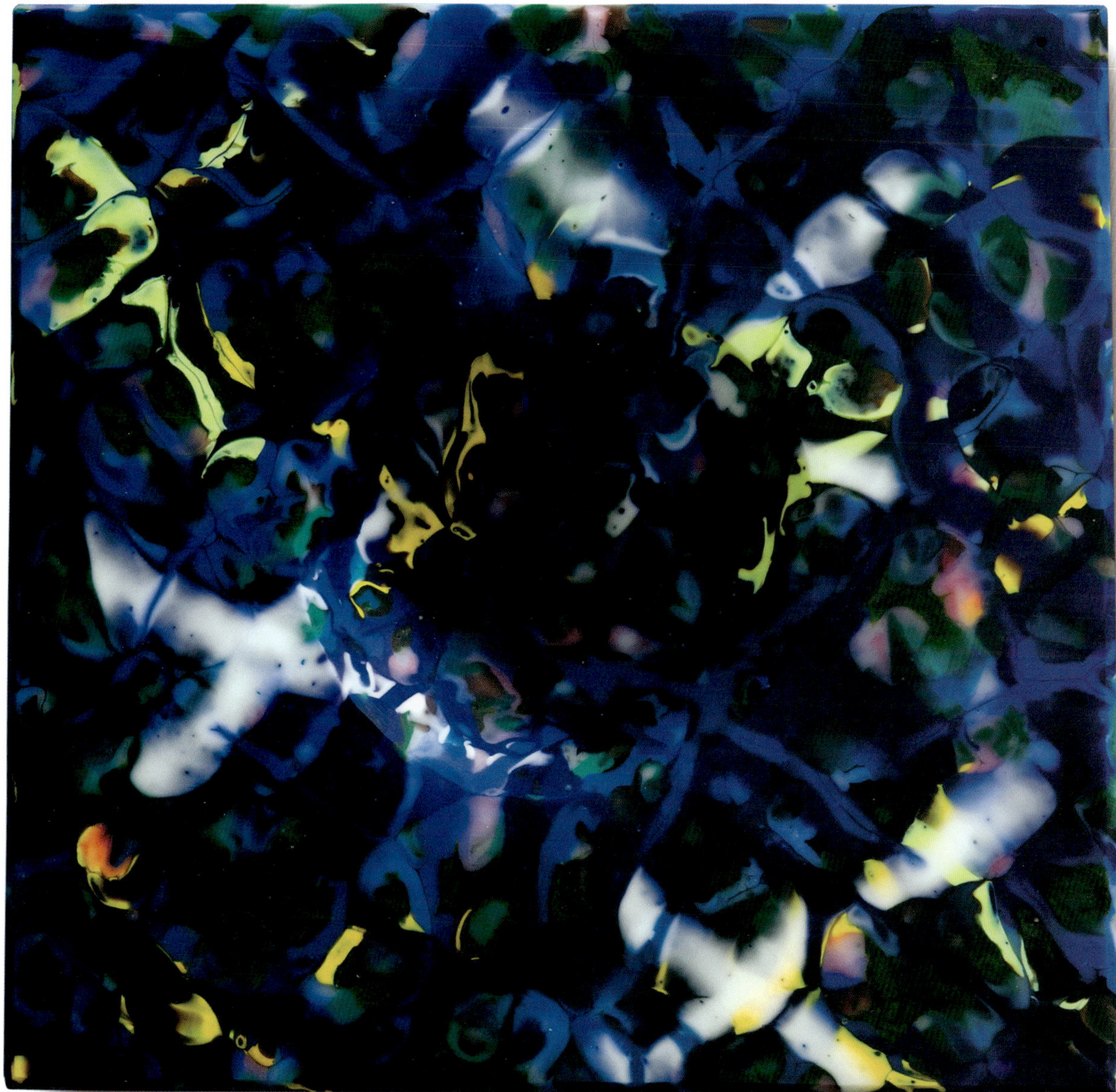

47. Untitled, 2000

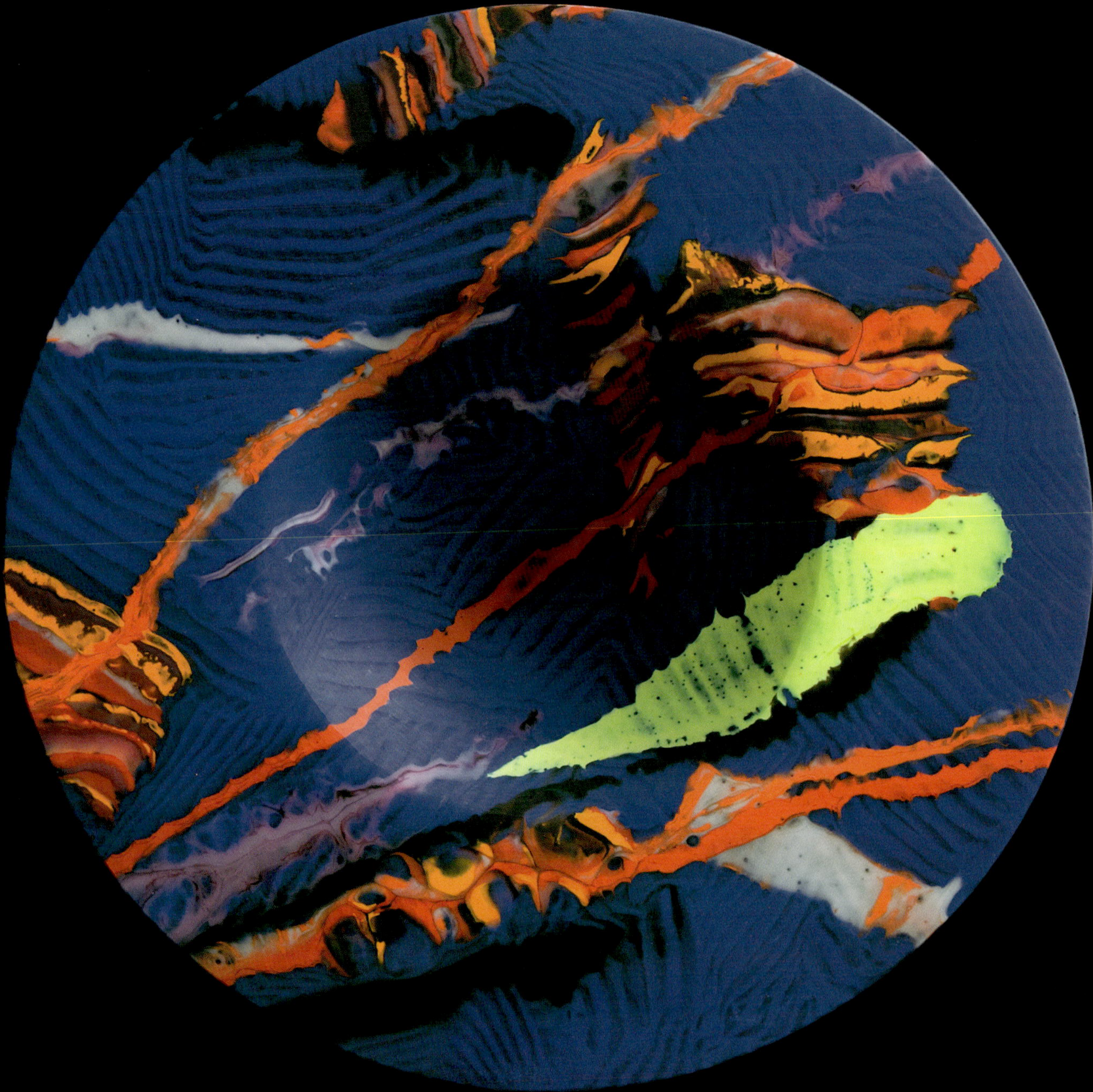

25. Untitled, 1989

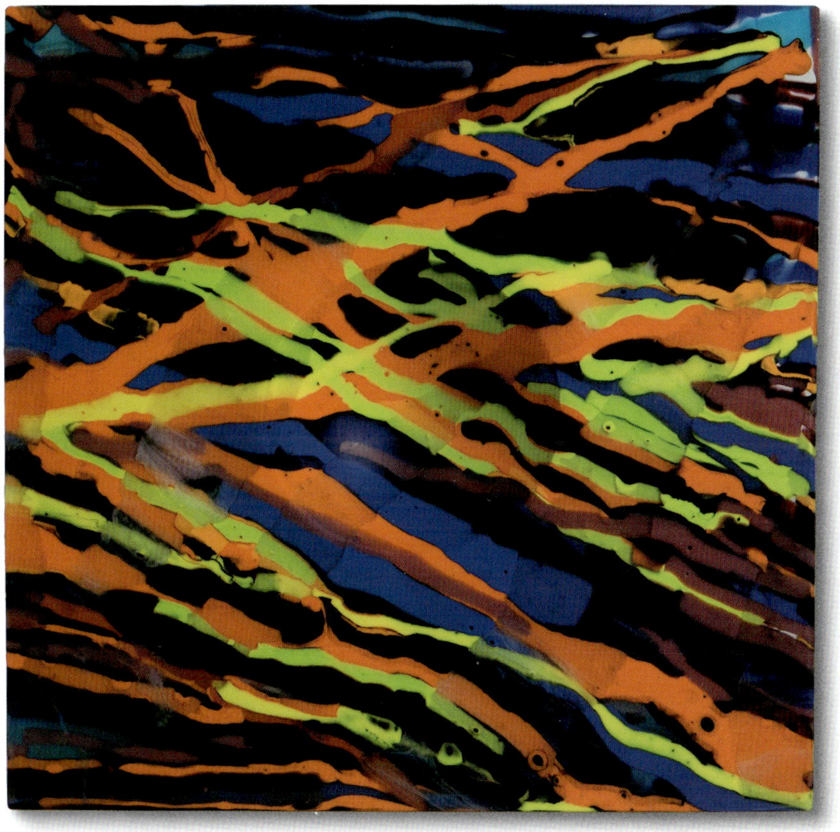

29. Untitled 7, 1990 (#31)

Around this time Moje decided to move away from "the restrictive atmosphere" in Germany, something he had become more aware of the more he travelled. He was at a high point in his career, but he felt the need for change. "My work was repetitive," he says. "I was working on a battery that was not reloading. Germany was not an option any more. I had reached a point where I asked, 'Where do I go from here?'"

Teaching interested him, but there were no suitable opportunities at home. He felt he wanted to give back through teaching what glass had given him as an artist. An invitation came just at the right moment, when he was asked by Udo Sellbach, director of the Canberra School of Art, to set up a glass course. In 1982 Moje moved to Australia with his partner, the ceramist Brigitte Enders.

Both teaching and his newly found freedom outside Germany transformed Moje's life. The workshop he set up in Canberra was unconventional for the time. He had made it clear to Sellbach that hot glass would not be the priority, which in a way came as welcome news because money was in short supply. Moje would begin by teaching cold-working techniques, his own speciality, and he made available his own workshop equipment to give the Canberra workshop a jump start until funding allowed for new equipment and an extension to hot glass.

He also insisted that the workshop have an independent faculty. He had seen how the hierarchy in schools where he had taught in America, Europe, and Japan had interfered with teaching aspirations. In his workshop, *skill* would not be a dirty word, as it was with some hot-glass pioneers who had downgraded skill's importance to a degree in favor of free conceptual thinking. As always, the tenet of *truth to materials* and the importance of craftsmanship formed the core of Moje's thinking, glass-making, and teaching.

Moje's own studio work developed dramatically after his move to Australia, especially in its shift to a more daring and dazzling color palette and the degree of technical sophistication, which was unmatched in any of his earlier work. Color had always been a stimulant for Moje, which he had started exploring in the mosaics. He noticed color everywhere and in everything that came into his field of vision. He was first struck by the emotional intensity of color when diving in the Gulf of Aqaba during the 1970s. A "plunge into a coral sea teeming with exotic fish delivered such an unexpected explosion of color and movement

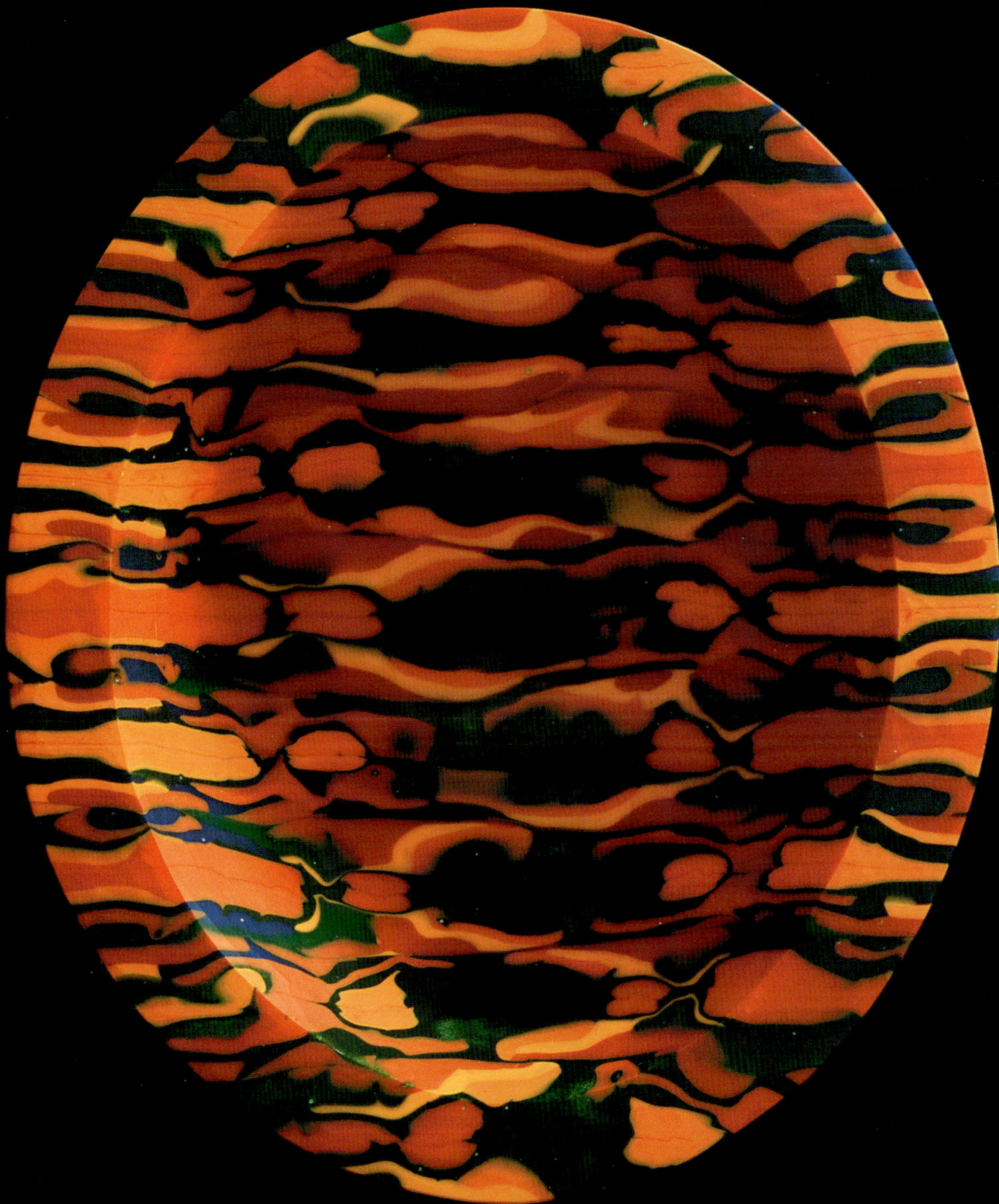

43. Untitled, 1997

that it left a profound and indelible impression on him."[iv] Now in Australia, Moje experienced the emotional effects of nature daily, "the amazing blue of the sky, the colors, the sounds, the birds, how the sound is carried in that environment." Brilliant daylight from dawn to dusk resulted in what seemed like a completely new color spectrum. He now compares the clear color separations he experienced to those seen in woodcuts.

Aboriginal art affected him deeply too, without influencing his work directly. On the occasion of receiving a Lifetime Achievement Award from the Glass Art Society of America in 2000, Moje said, "Australian aboriginal art has certainly been an inspiration for me. The quality I admire most about it, I think, is the connection between nature and their expression…I have not taken aspects of Aboriginal art from the Aborigines—I transferred what I experienced in their art into something else. This is something deep in my heart: this art gives me the power, I would say, to use colors, or precisely to feel color in a different way."[v]

Recalling the technical challenges at that time, Moje says, "Glass is very restrictive and unforgiving. It is difficult to break through given

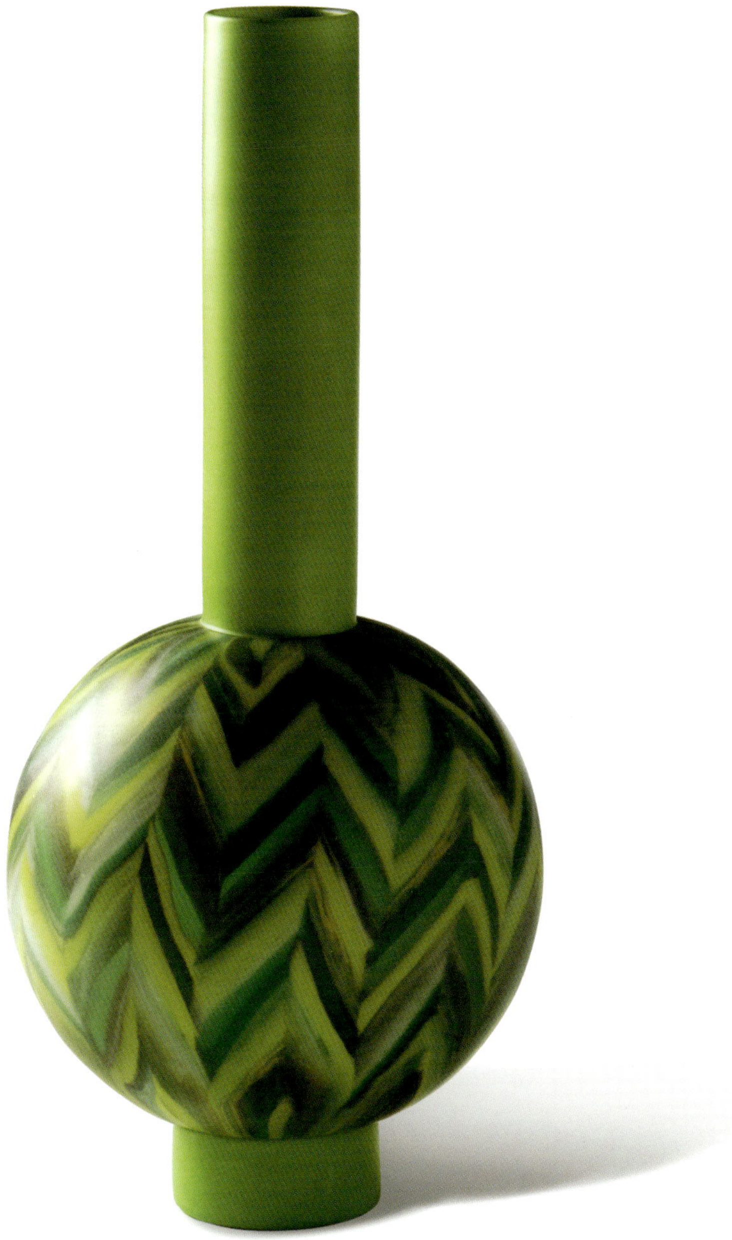

35. M/M/P-4, 1993 (#33)

barriers and resolve problems. There is always a struggle between inspiration and realization: so pushing that envelope has always been with me. I try to achieve the impossible within my limitations." Fortunately, an outside force had recently stepped in to help him achieve "the impossible." He had developed a relationship with Bullseye Glass Company, and in particular with Dan Schwoerer, whose life has been devoted to finding solutions to color compatibility in glass, thereby transforming the glass artist's color palette.

After Moje started using Bullseye glass he never looked back. His collaboration with this company became one of the most important in the story of contemporary glass. It meant that for the first time, glass sheet, as opposed to glass cane, could be used for fusing. Says Moje, "Being able to arrange the glass using sheet and not cane gave great scope for a new design aesthetic, as did the wider range of colors available."[vi] Dan Schwoerer says, "Klaus brought credibility to Bullseye. He inspired me in a manner that said, 'Wow—this is something that world-class artists could use.'"[vii]

Both Schwoerer and Moje were committed to research and education and to the link between

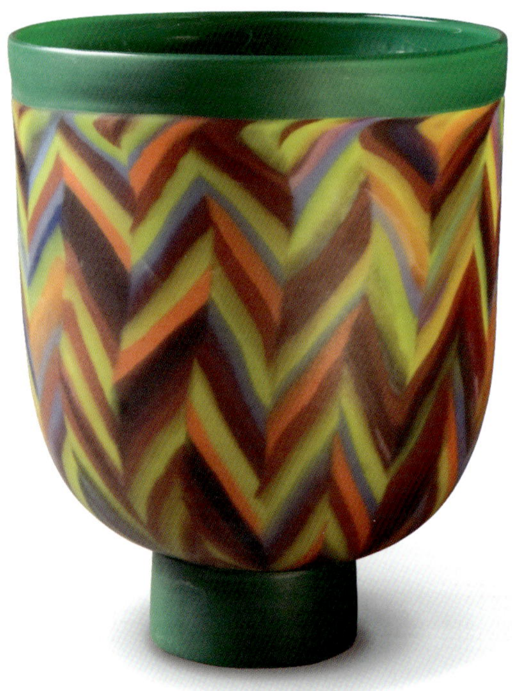

34. M/M/P-4, 1993 (#43)

artistic creation and industrial invention. Through Moje, Bullseye developed an important relationship with the Canberra School of Art. Three years after Moje stopped teaching at the school, Bullseye co-owner Lani McGregor worked with Kirstie Rea, one of Moje's students (and now artistic director of the newly opened Canberra Glassworks), to "keep the research rolling" and "to involve an emerging generation in the project,"[viii] Two workshops resulted, one in 1995 and the other in 1997, working with blowers and kilnformers in Australia. The projects were called *Latitudes*, and the first culminated in an exhibition that travelled to Portland in the summer of 1995 to inaugurate the new Bullseye Connection Gallery.

Moje's involvement with Bullseye also led to a number of collaborative projects, notably with glassblowers Billy Morris at Pilchuck (1987) and Dante Marioni in Portland (1993). It led less directly to the development of a new glass-working method, called the *Great Australian Rollup,* with former students Scott Chaseling and Kirstie Rea.

All of these projects resulted in experimental work that has a place in Moje's oeuvre. For the project with Dante Marioni, "Moje came prepared with fused mosaic sheets he had made in Australia. The team successfully made a series of blown mosaic vessels, signed M/M/P (Moje/Marioni/Portland)."[ix] The prelude to the Great Australian Rollup was an invitation to be master-in-residence at the 10th Niijima International Glass Art Festival at the Niijima Glass Center in Japan. With his usual daredevil approach, Moje decided upon arriving to respond to the "Edo period textiles that had enthralled him during the previous day's stopover in Tokyo."[x]

His time at Niijima was short, and the six vessels he made suffered annealing problems, but the experiment led to his spectacular *Niijima* series. In these pieces, Moje fused colored glasses into patterned slabs through the course of several firings in a kiln, cooling and grinding the slabs, and then reheating them. The process made the slabs malleable enough to be picked up and wrapped—or rolled up—around a disc of clear glass on the end of a blowpipe to form a cylinder. The open end of this cylinder was then closed to form a bubble, which was subsequently blown and manipulated. The result was patterning in the round that had the softness and depth of fabric.

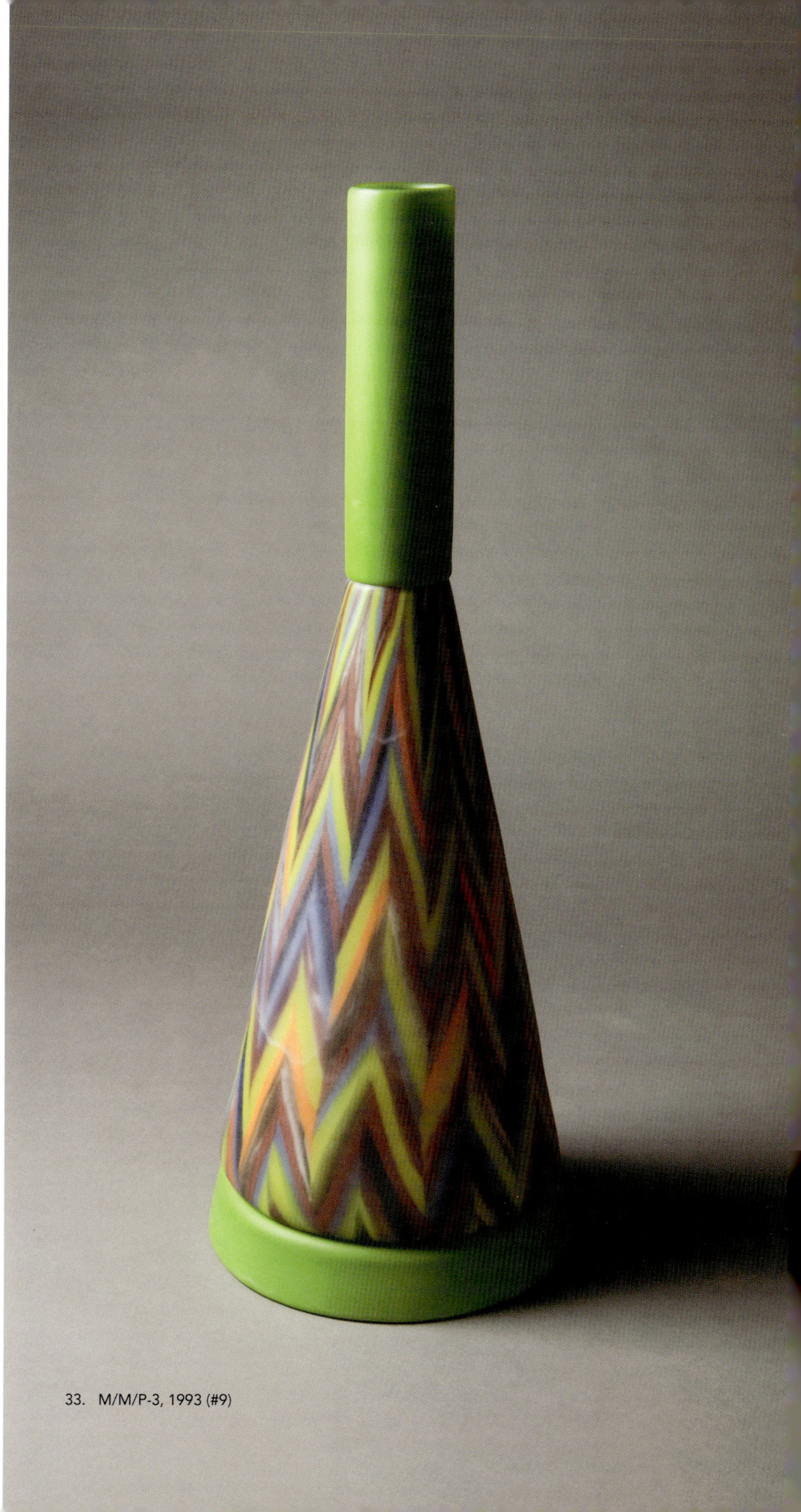

33. M/M/P-3, 1993 (#9)

Such collaborations were an important aspect of Moje's development as an artist. They were also diversions from which he benefited greatly when he returned to his own work. Starting with the *New Horizon* series in the 1980s, Moje's palette became more saturated, richer, and painterly. In the first *New Horizon* pieces he still clung to linear geometry, but the work was noticeably freer, more psychedelic in color. If the lines were wavy, this stemmed partly from the fact that Bullseye was still in the process of perfecting color compatibility, so some of the colored strips reacted differently to kiln temperatures. But this technical accident only added to Moje's new sense of freedom. Increasingly, straight lines dissolved into much more expressionistic effects that at times resembled the random (but controlled) color compositions of marbled paper.

Inspired by the sights and sounds of Australia and emboldened by increased technical security, Moje's colors now lept at viewers with an intensity not seen in his previous work. During this time he also experimented with new shapes, split forms, box forms, shield shapes, and the series he called *Songlines*. These experiments were something he felt the need to do, but on his own admission plane was more important to him than form. "I don't see forms—bowls, bowls

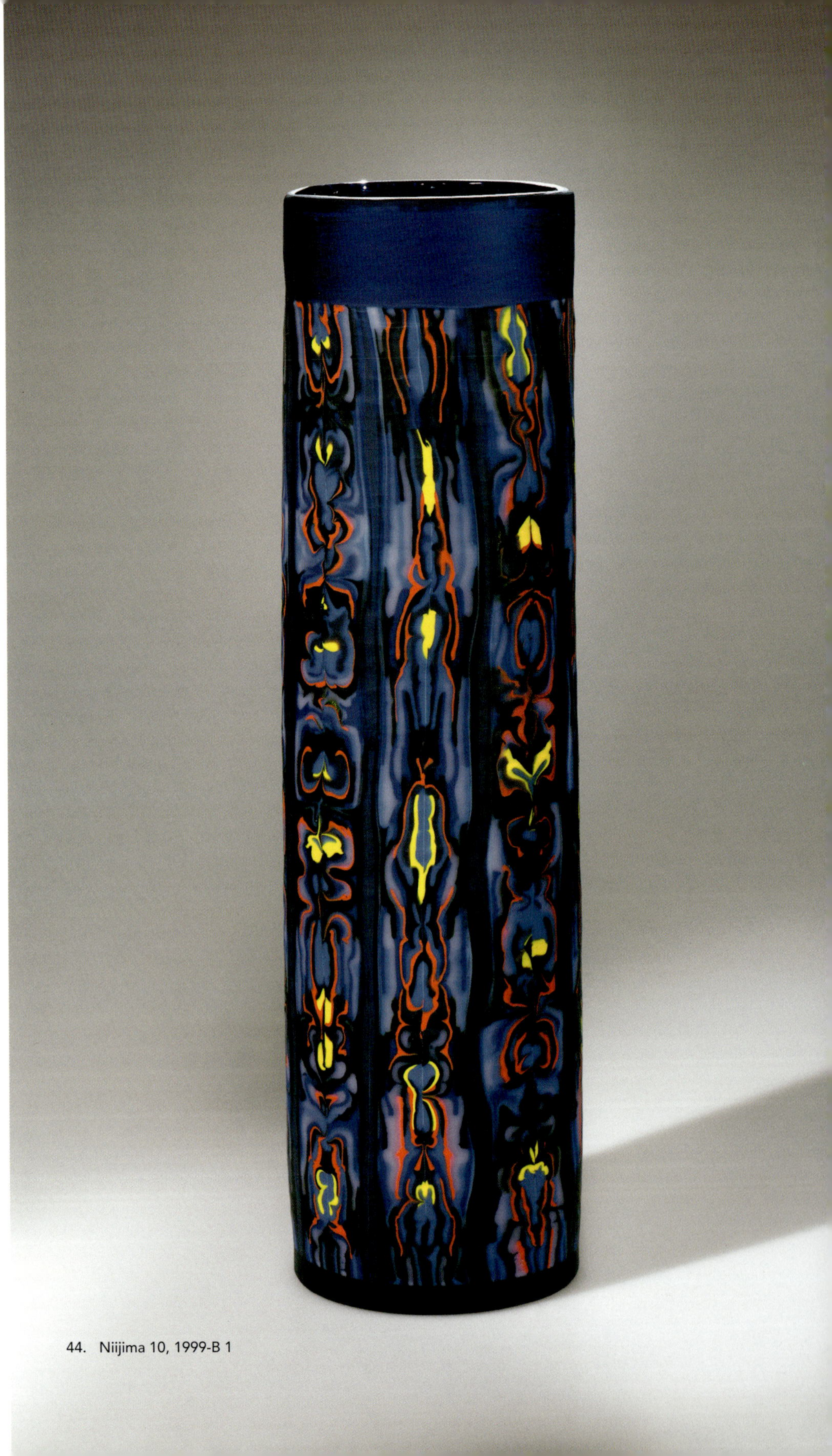

44. Niijima 10, 1999-B 1

with collars, boxes, plates, wall pieces—as a classification in my work. My work is mainly about plane."

Moje's shift from vessel to wall first occurred in 1996 with an invitation to exhibit at the Palazzo Ducale in Venice during the festival of new glass, *Venezia Aperto Vetro*. He had long considered how a shift to flat art might work for him, whether it would bring greater freedom in some way. His *Aperto* piece was a wall panel composed of sixteen square glass tiles, where liquid reds and blacks were punctuated by enriching yellows with accents of blue. The piece engaged viewers in a new way. It was no longer an object but had all the power one associates with a painting.

The shift from three to two dimensions had a marked effect on all of Moje's work, adding depth to his color palette and liberating him from the confining rigors of vessel forms. His attitude toward composition shifted from decoration to construction. The patterning of his color fields became more architectural, the geometry appearing almost three-dimensional. This greater sense of dissonance brought additional emotion to the work, even if it was always tempered by calculated balance.

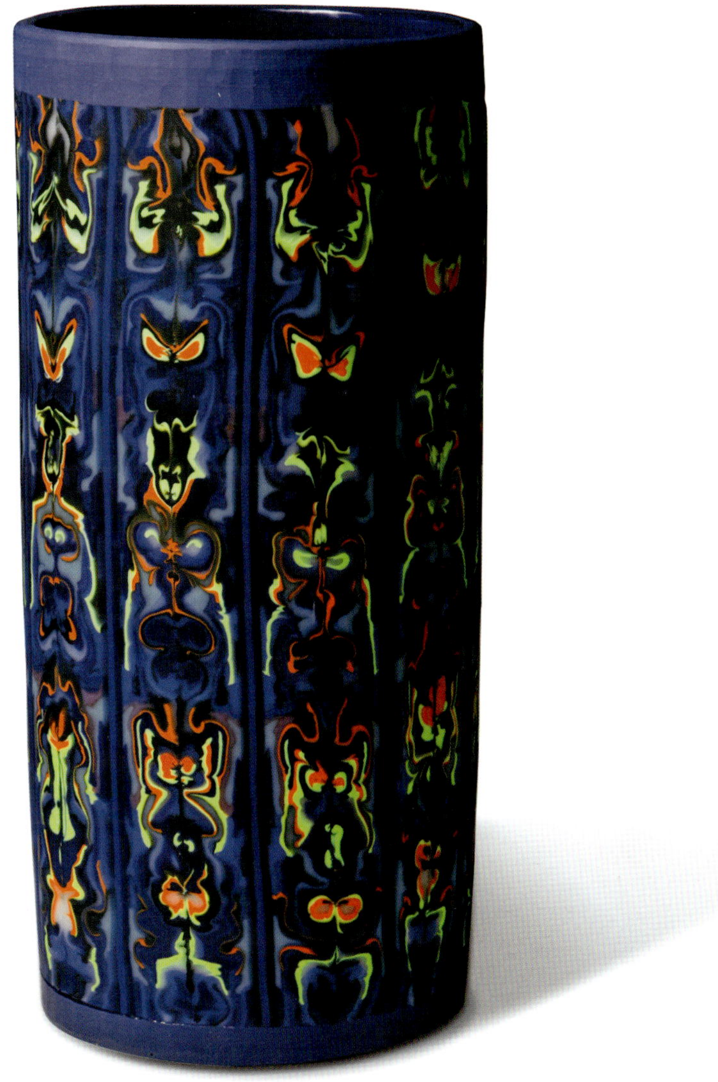

45. Niijima, 2000

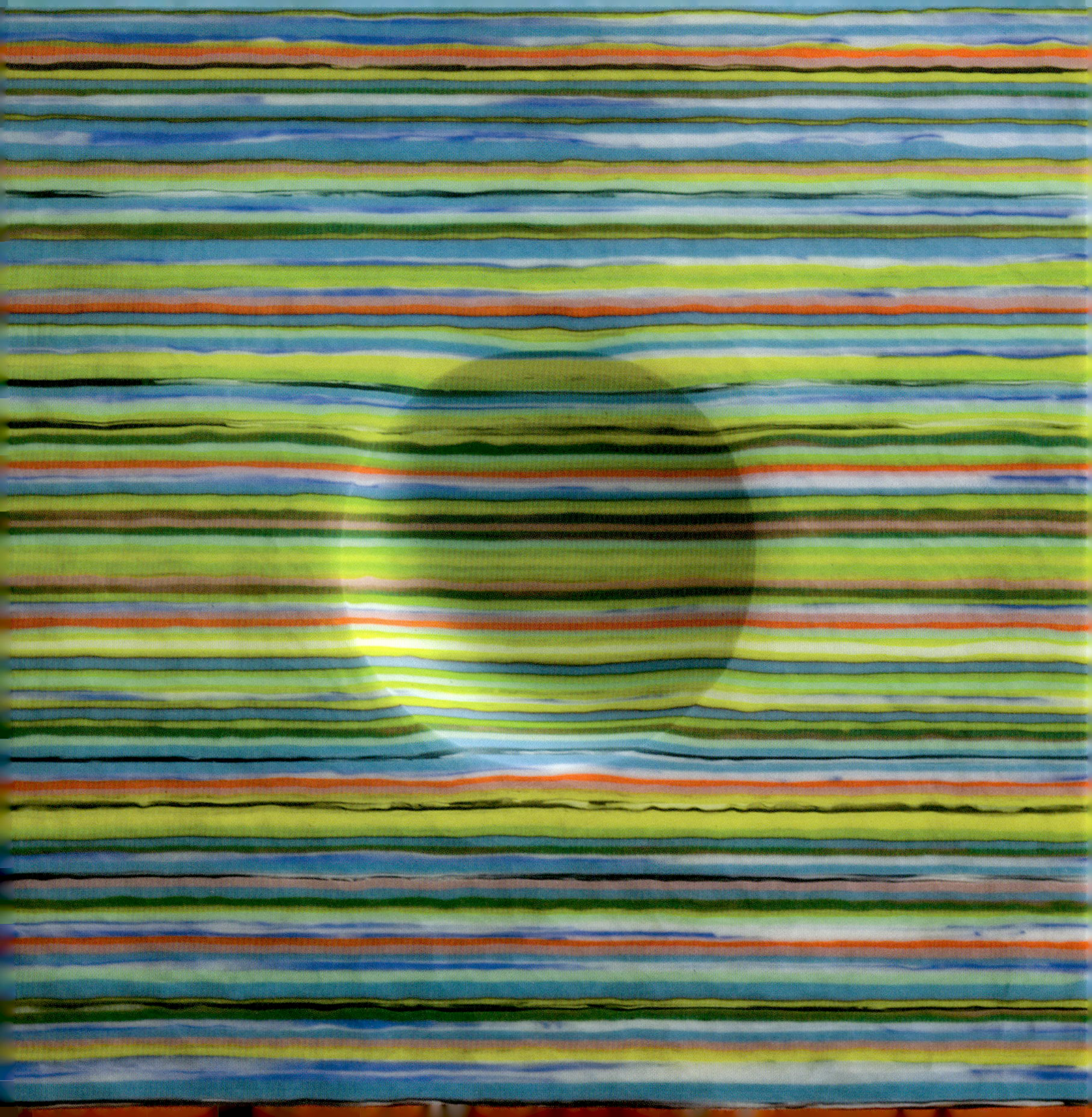

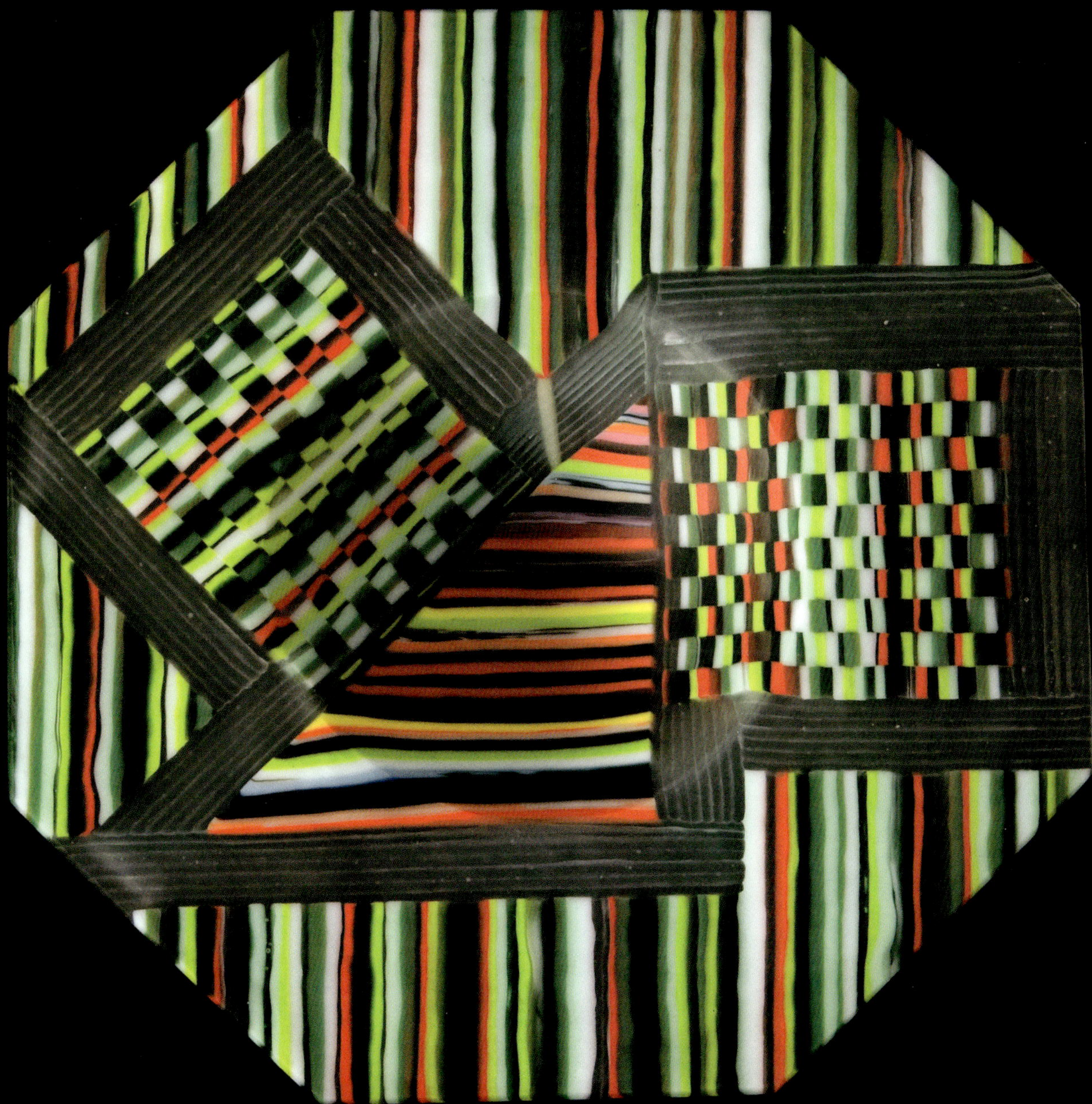

37. Untitled 1, 1984 (#2)

In 1998 Moje produced another wall panel in sixteen sections for a commission for the Australian Legislative Assembly in Canberra. Emotion was evident even in Moje's brief about the commission, which stated that his piece should remind the legislative powers that they occupied Aboriginal land: "When I see an Aboriginal painting, I see a whole different world that is articulated in the unbelievable—eyes which reflect their heritage, their present predicament, and their spirituality. It is in their paintings that these things come together."

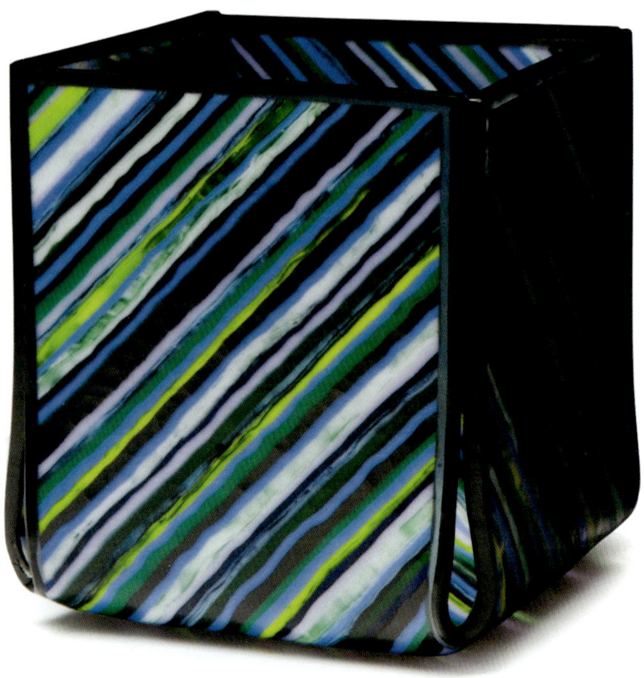

32. Untitled, c. 1993

As Moje continued working in flat planes, the lines in his work collapsed and became more deconstructed and the composition more complex. The colors grew more fragmented, the expression more emotive, the choreography more reasoned. These qualities are particularly noticeable in pieces that date from the new century, which have fearless color combinations that fight one another yet always remain well behaved, tempered by a sense of *Deutsche Ordnung*—German sense of order—that will always be present in the artist's make up.

Never content to rest on his laurels, Moje was excited by the challenge of a retrospective exhibition at the Portland Art Museum. The

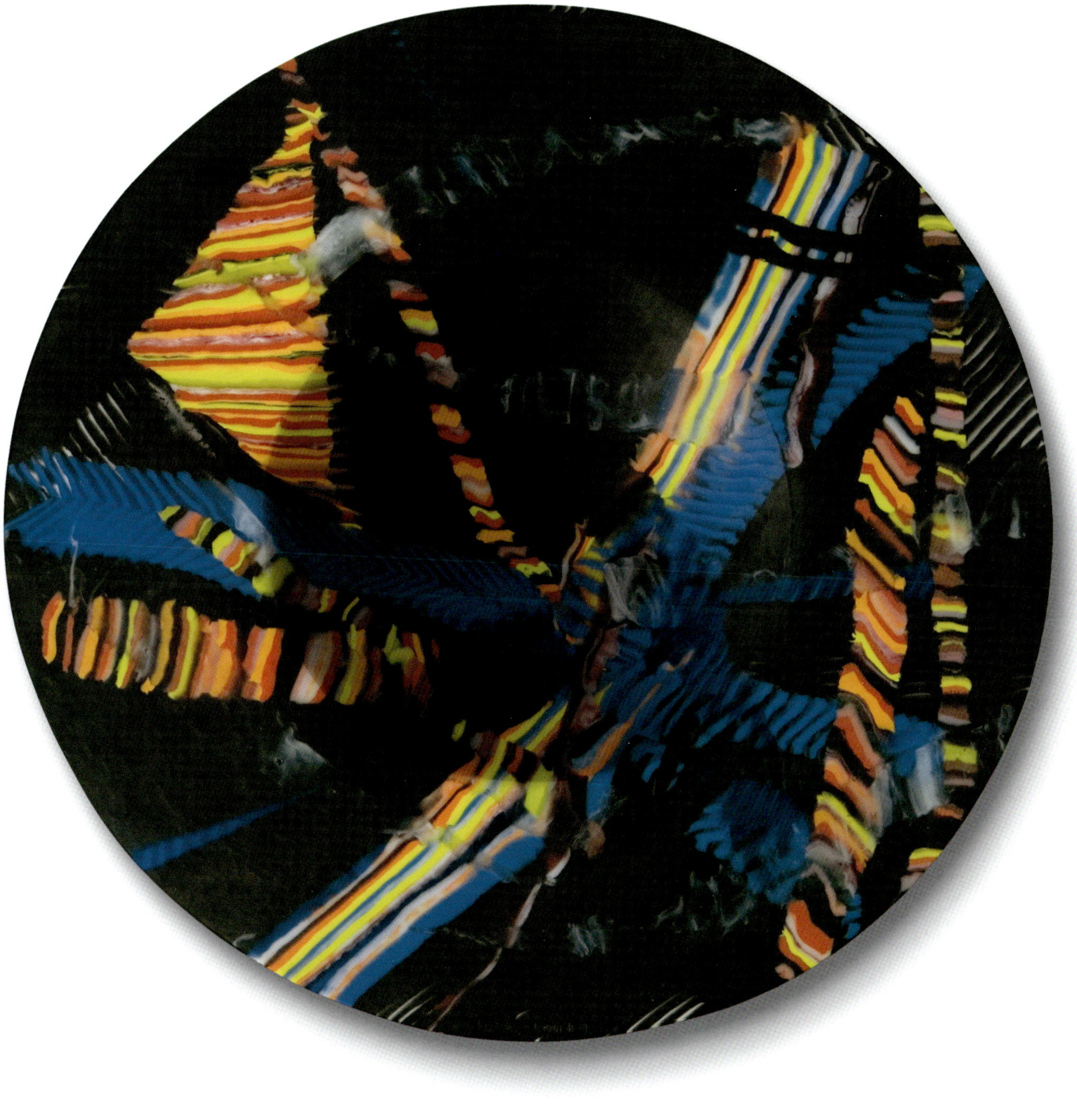

30. Untitled, 1991 (#19)

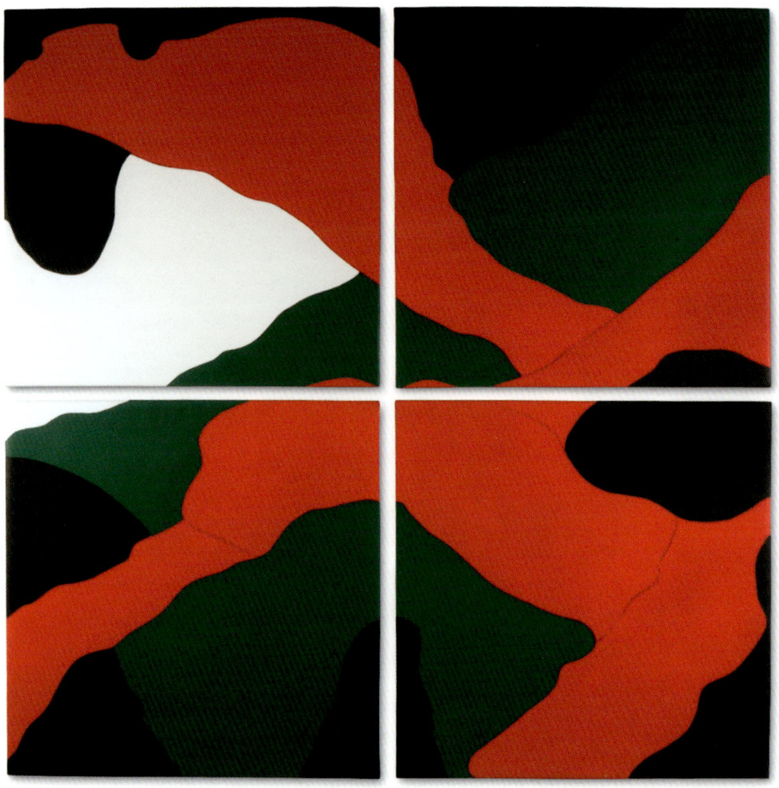

46. Floating Red, 2000

exhibition is in many ways the culmination of his collaboration with Bullseye and a tribute to the positive response he has enjoyed in the United States for nearly forty years. The museum's curator, Bruce Guenther, told Bullseye, "We need one big work here," indicating that the exhibition needed a major focal point and a dynamic but not overwhelming presence for the back wall. Lani McGregor and Dan Schwoerer passed on the message when they met with Moje in Los Angeles to choose pieces for the Portland exhibition from Dan Greenberg and Susan Steinhauser's collection. There was an exhibition of German paintings at the Getty Museum at the time. Moje stood in front of two large-scale gray paintings by Gerhard Richter and said, "I thought I would like to capture the dimension of these paintings in my work." In the end, his answer was to make a suite of panels, "a group of four that spoke as one."

Because of its scale this work had to be made in Portland. There were no kilns large enough in Australia to accommodate the panels, each of which measures 74 1/2 by 47 1/4 inches (189 by 120 cm). Moje worked with a team of young artists and technicians from Bullseye, most of them in their twenties. Making the piece involved cutting thousands of color strips that would be

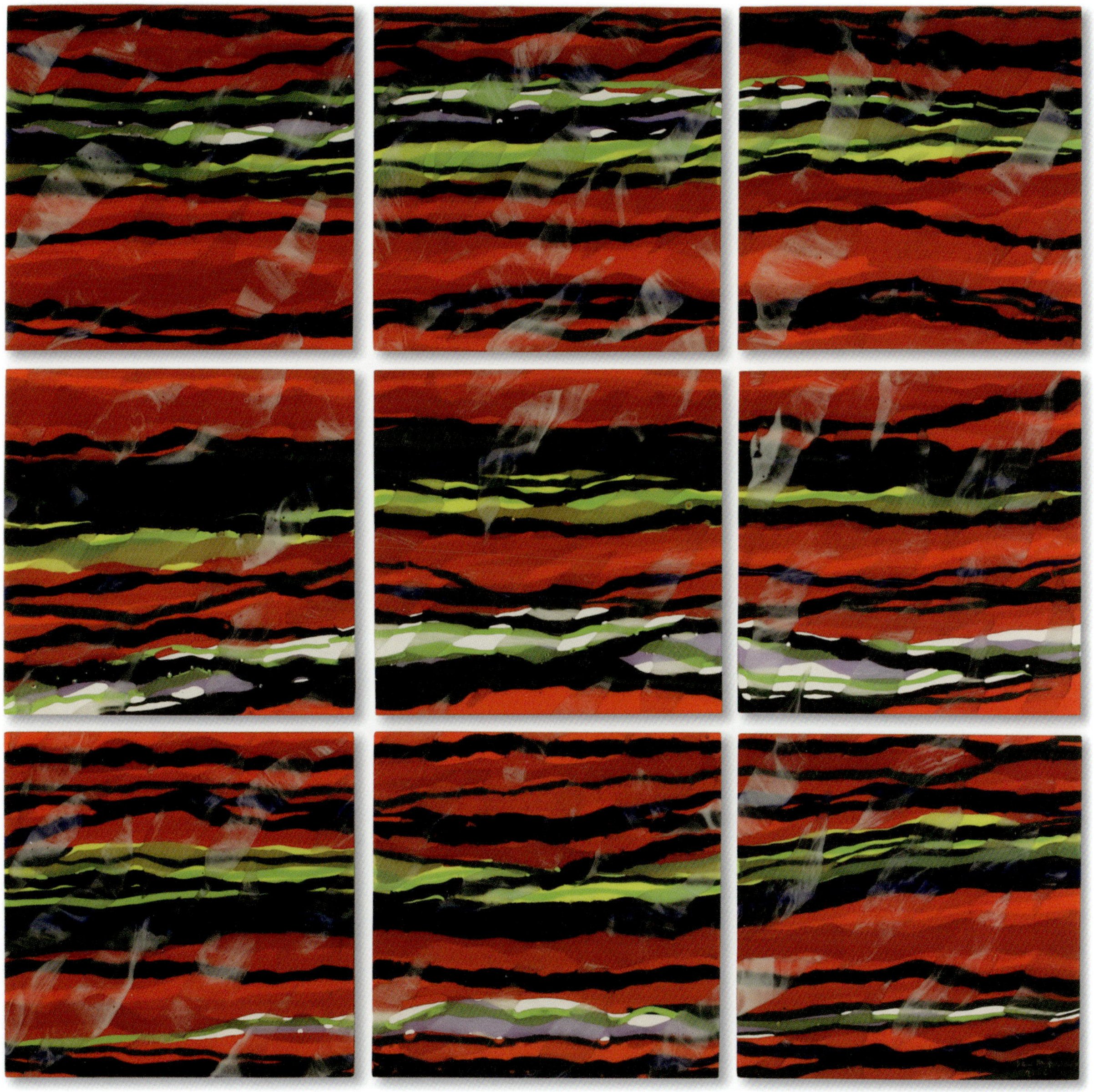

63. Untitled 2, 2006

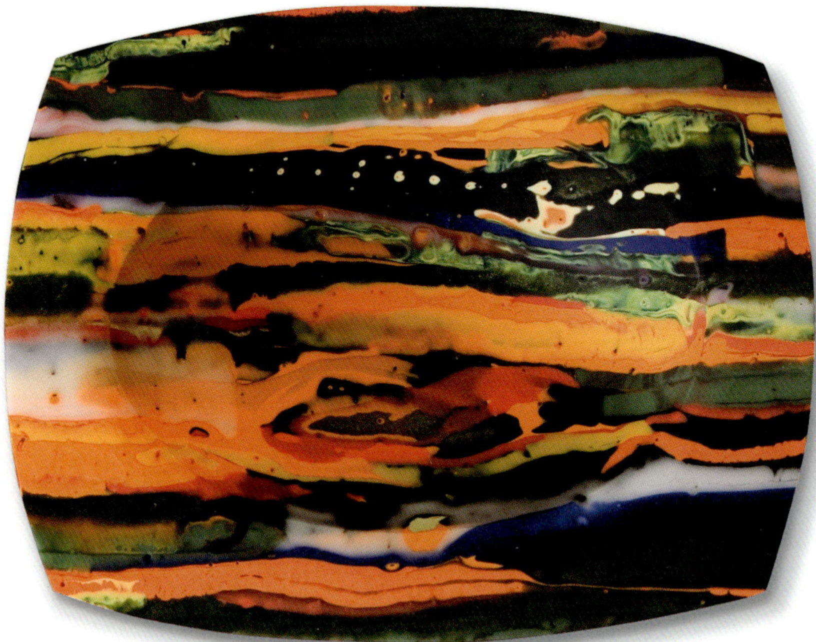

38. Untitled, 1995

spread in bold linear stripes across the whole composition. Smaller panels composed of colored strips cut from sheet were laid out in a polychrome arrangement and fired in a kiln. These were then cut up on a diamond saw to make a variety of different shapes, which were laid out as in a jigsaw puzzle to form the larger panels. Each component segment had to be cut to a required shape and size. When the composition was finished, the four panels were transported to the kiln, and a two-and-a-half-week firing schedule was set in motion.

Moje is both a team leader and hands-on collaborator from start to finish—a quality that has endeared him to all the professionals and students with whom he has worked. The team of young Bullseye assistants was impressed by his knowledge of what the material can and cannot do and by his decisive way of working and organizational abilities. One must emphasize here that Moje's knowledge and skill embody the accumulation of fifty years of adventurous and passionate technical experiment, half of it during his years in Germany, the other half in collaboration with Bullseye. Neither portion alone could have achieved such results.

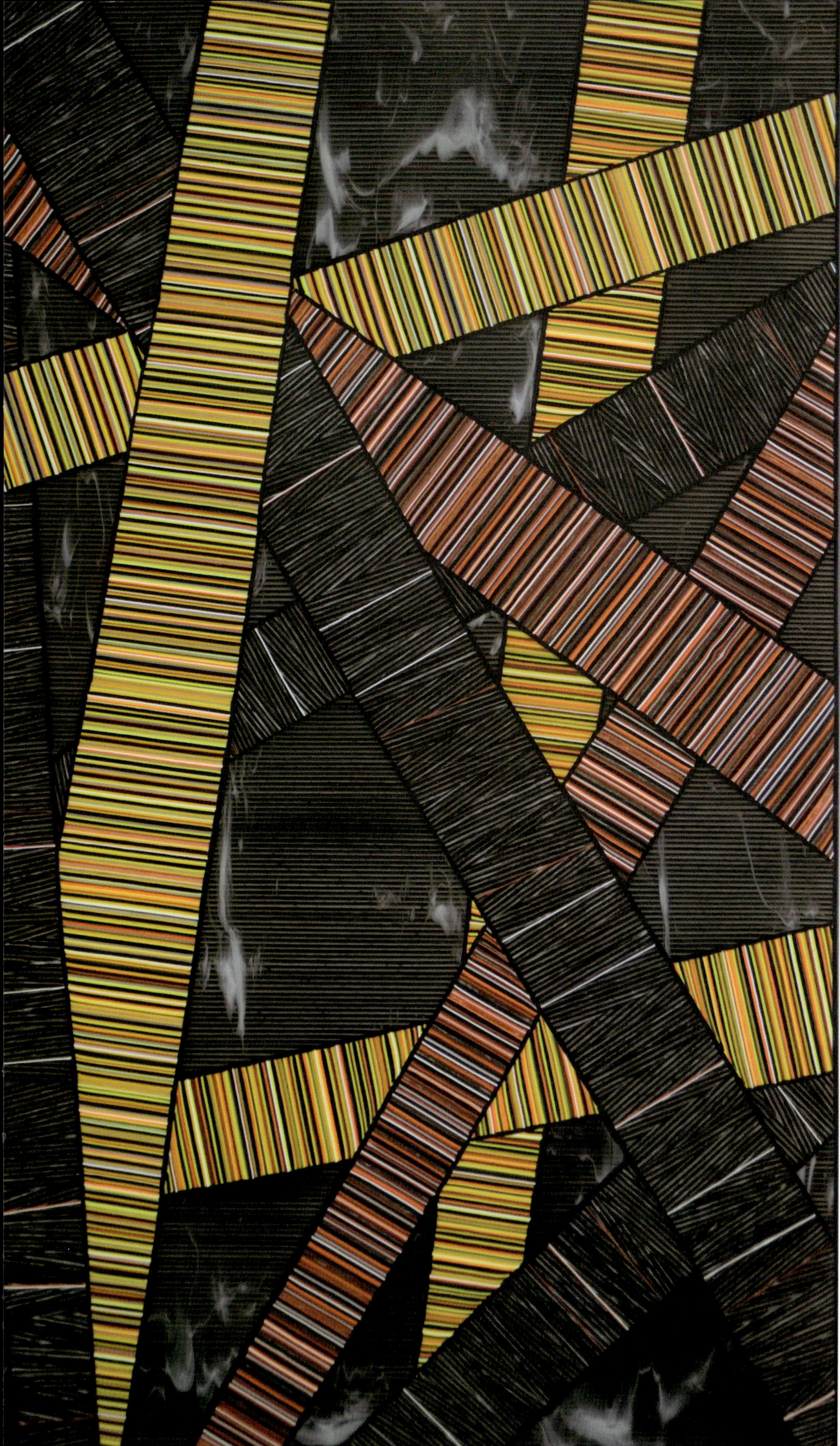

67. The Portland Panels: Choreographed Geometry, 2007
(Detail)

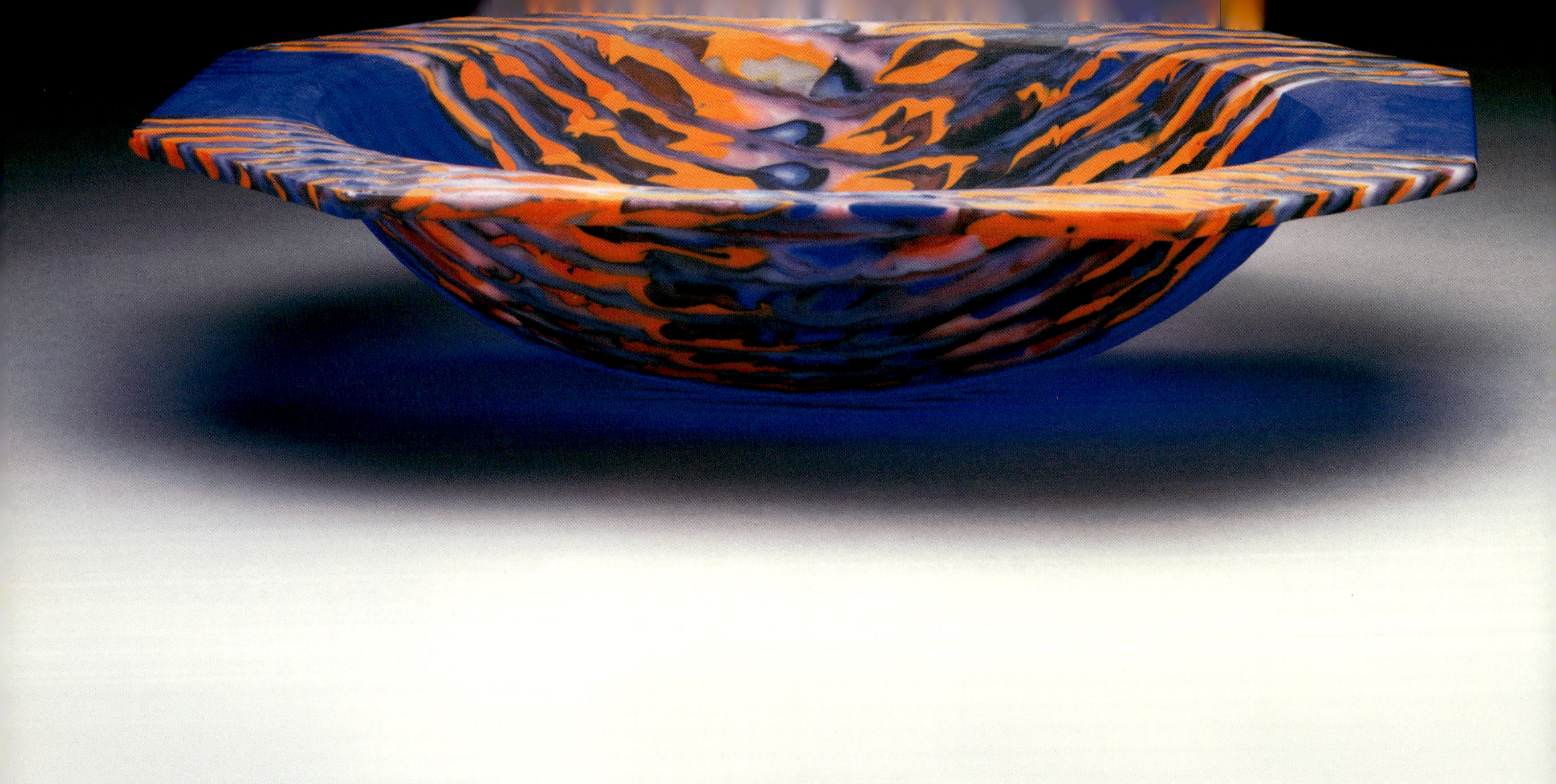

39. Untitled, 1995 (#48)

Choreographed Geometry 2007 must count as one of the most important works of the artist's career. Its completion is a crowning glory of his technical achievements, but it also opens a new world of architectural possibilities for Moje. The constructed polychrome imagery follows logically from what he has done in the past, but it also marks the beginning of new thinking. Working on such a large scale alters many perceptions, and it is a measure of Moje's talent that he was able to make the leap. For those who first saw the four panels together, fresh out of the kiln, the impact was "stunning." The color pyrotechnics and dancing lines were "intoxicating." On that occasion the panels were simply propped against a wall, but viewers were already able to sense the excitement that the work will generate as the centerpiece in Moje's retrospective exhibition everywhere it is seen in the United States.

Many artists and students have benefited from Klaus Moje's long journey in glass. Numerous important creators who work in fused glass owe him an enormous debt of gratitude. His combination of material understanding and polychrome splendor have made a significant contribution to contemporary art. Nothing can better express why than Moje's own words, as

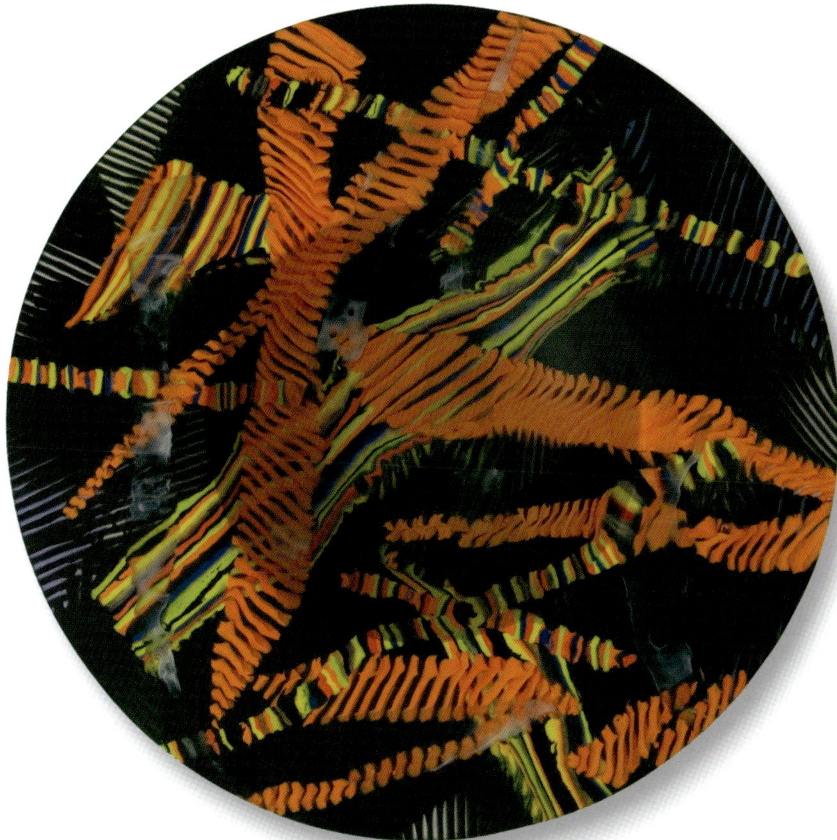

40. Untitled, 1995 (#6)

always spoken straight from the heart: "I believe glass loves me. My whole life has circled around this wonderful material…I know my focus is glass and will always be glass. This is my choice. This is my material, and I am in love with it."[xi] ■

[i] Unless otherwise noted, quotations from the artist are from the author's conversation with Klaus Moje in Portland, Oregon, July 2007.

[ii] Frank Whitford, *Bauhaus* (London: Thames & Hudson, 1984), 12.

[iii] Cited in conversation with Klaus Moje, Portland, Oregon, July 2007.

[iv] Megan Bottari, *Klaus Moje Glass* (Australia: Object & Craftsman House, 2006), 21.

[v] *The Glass Art Society Journal* (Seattle: Glass Art Society, 2000), 51.

[vi] Merryn Gates, *Latitudes: Bullseye Glass in Australia* (Canberra: Canberra School of Art, 2000), 6.

[vii] In conversation with Dan Schwoerer, Portland , Oregon, July 2007

[viii] Kirstie Rea, *Latitudes: Bullseye Glass in Australia* (Canberra: Canberra School of Art, 2000), 6.

[ix] Gates, 6.

[x] Bottari, 94.

[xi] *The Glass Art Society Journal*, 51.

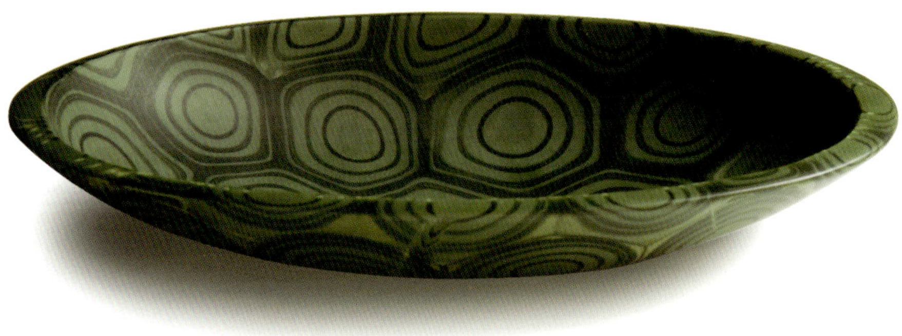

4. Untitled 5, 1977

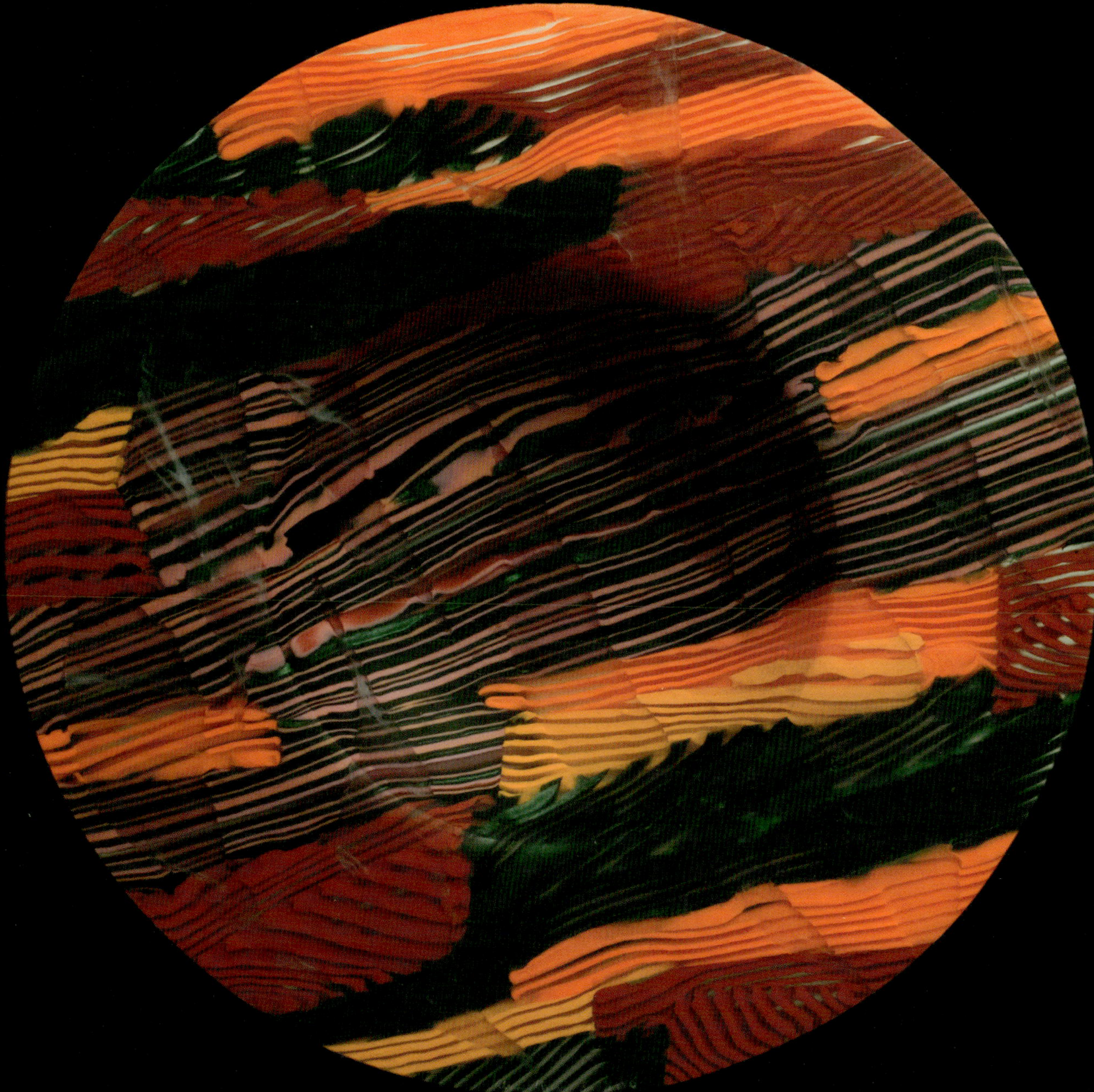

60. Untitled 3, 2006

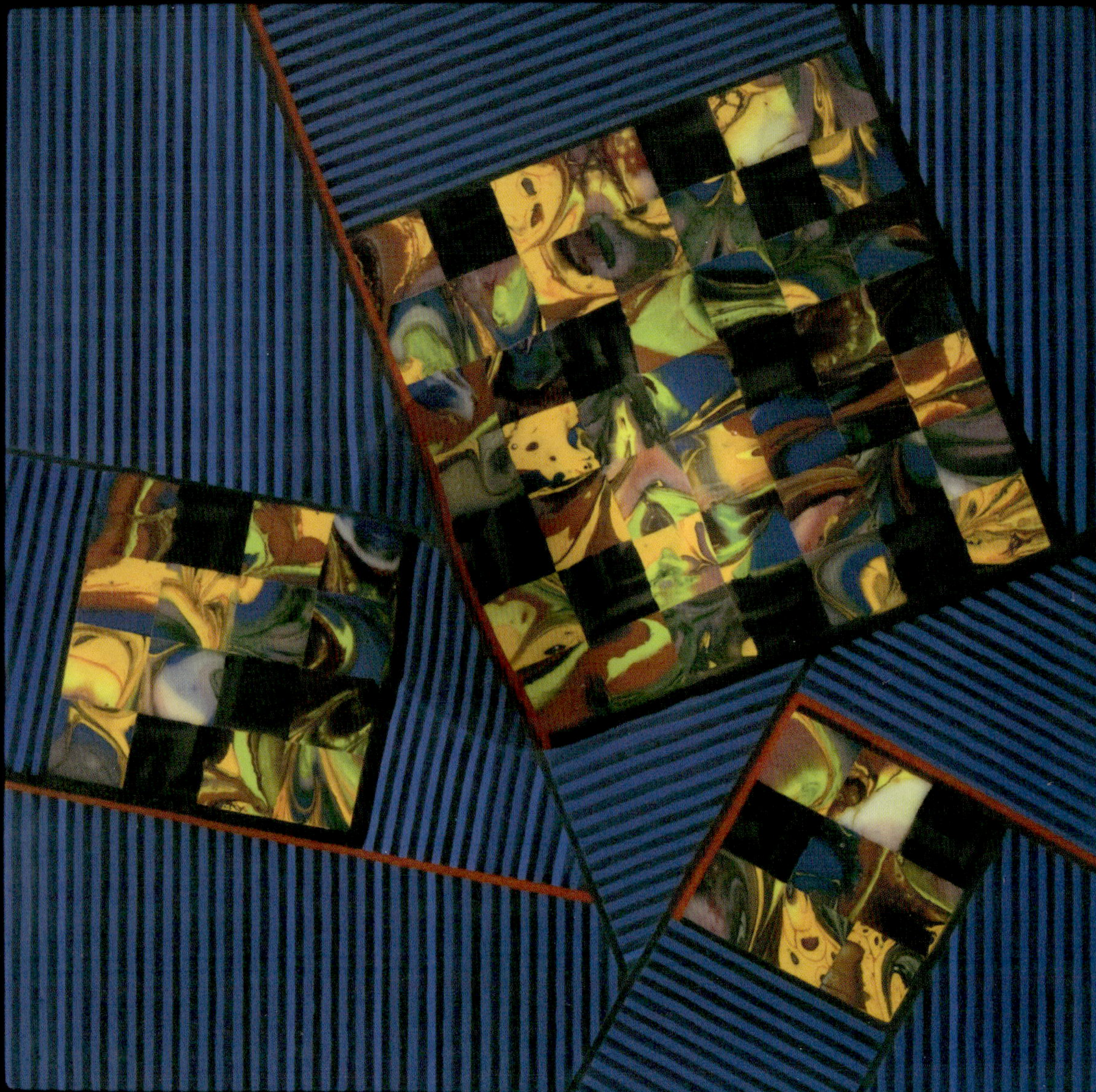

26. Untitled, 1989

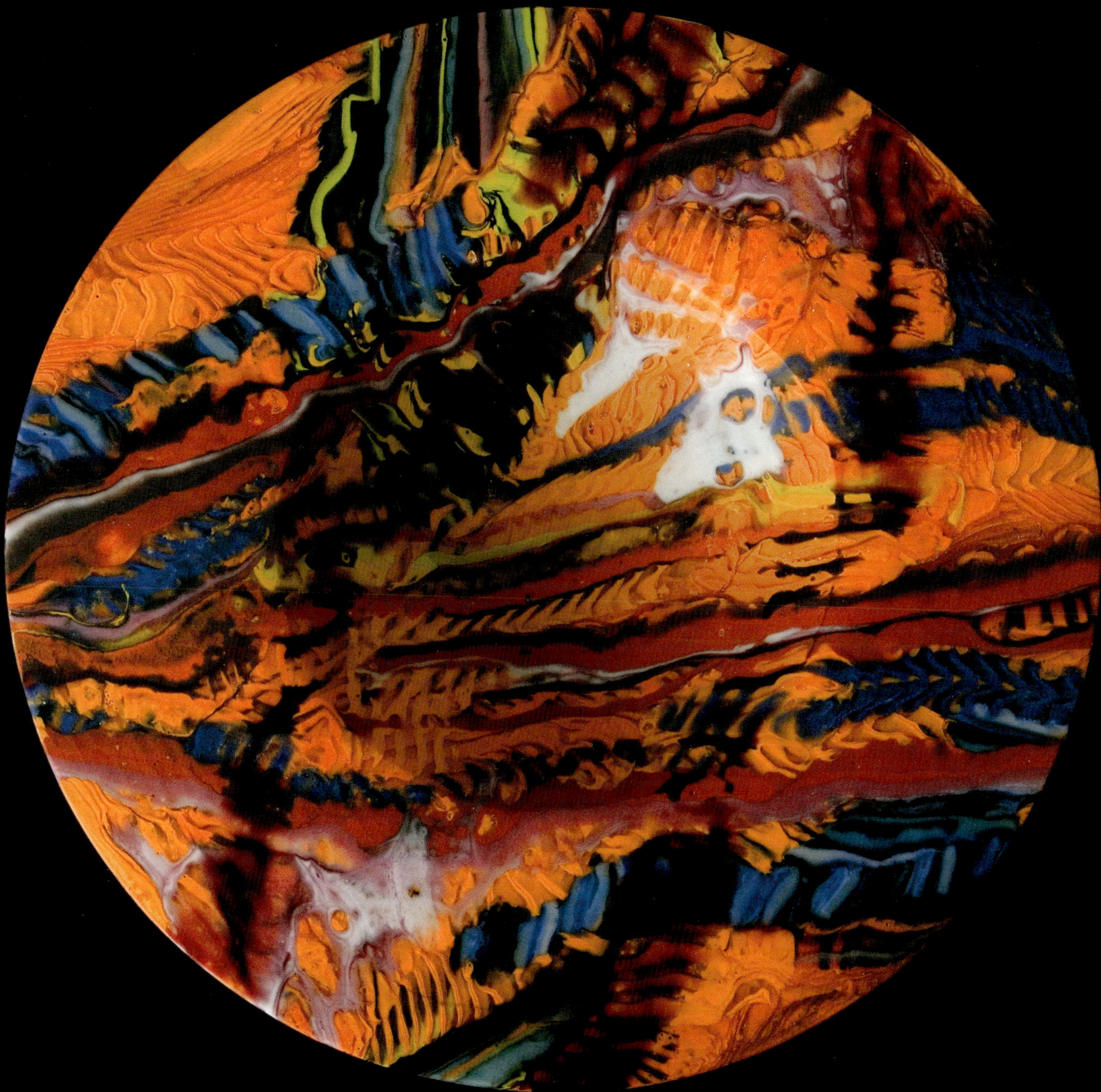

27. Untitled 1, 1990 (#2)

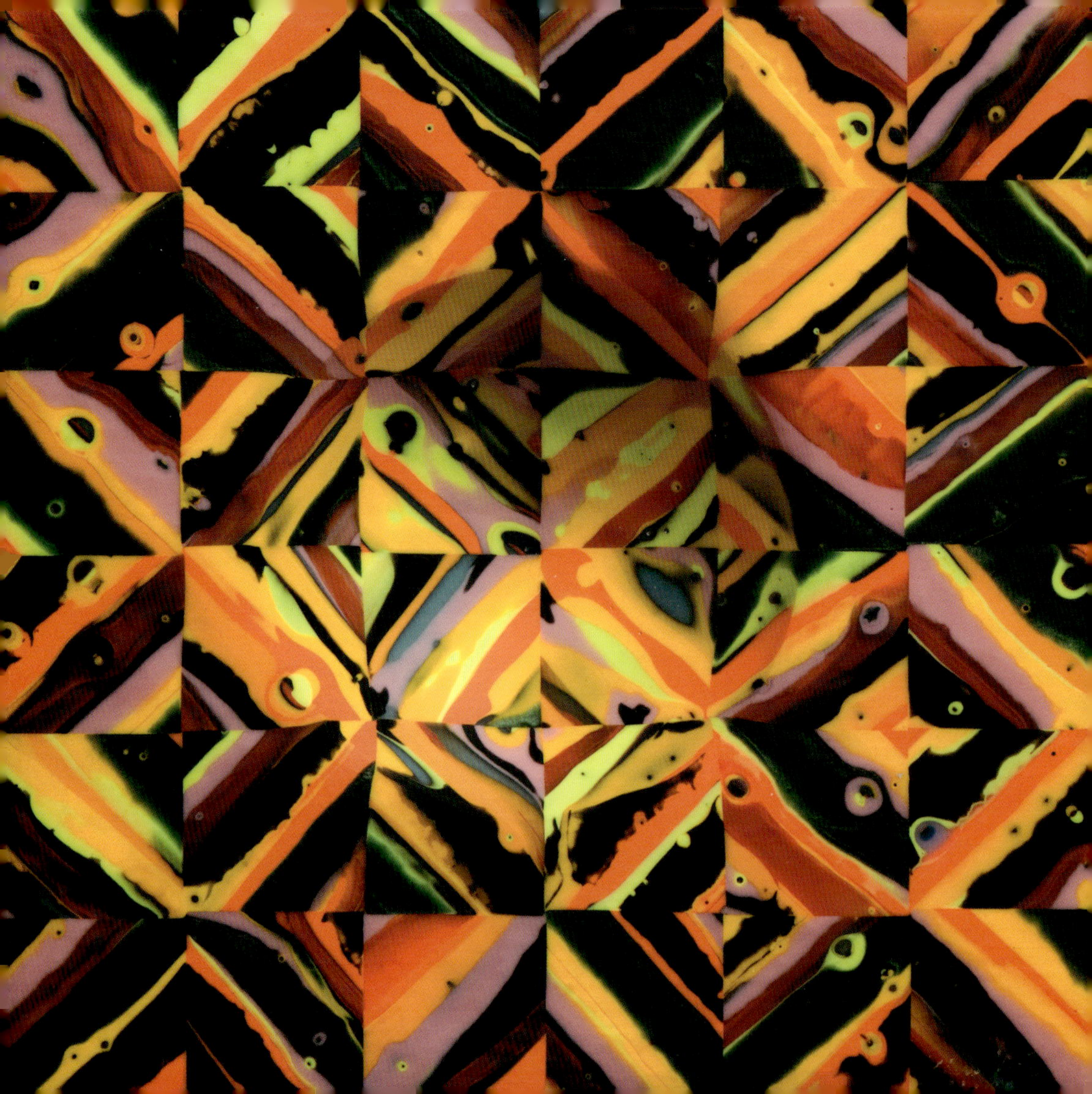

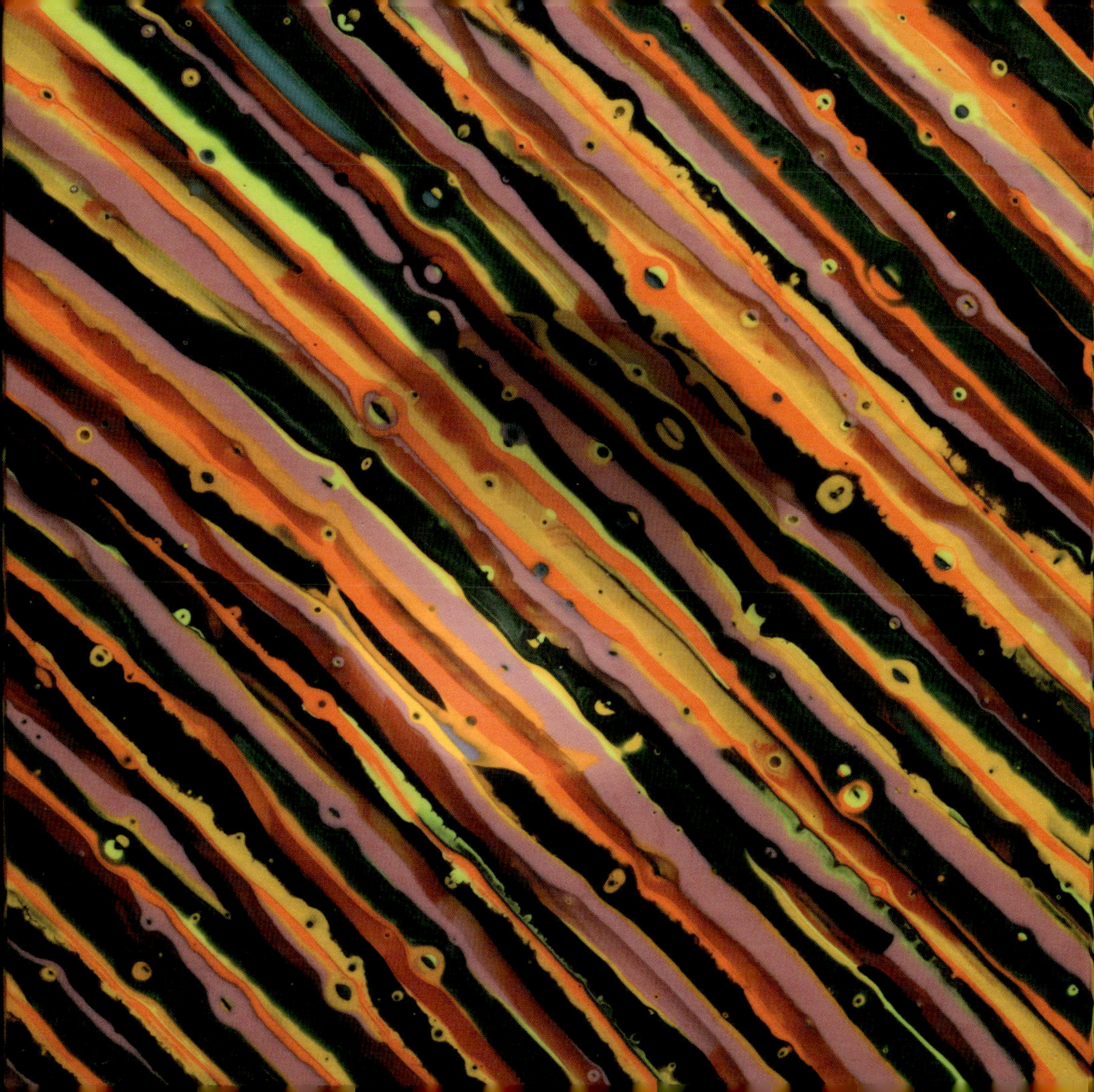

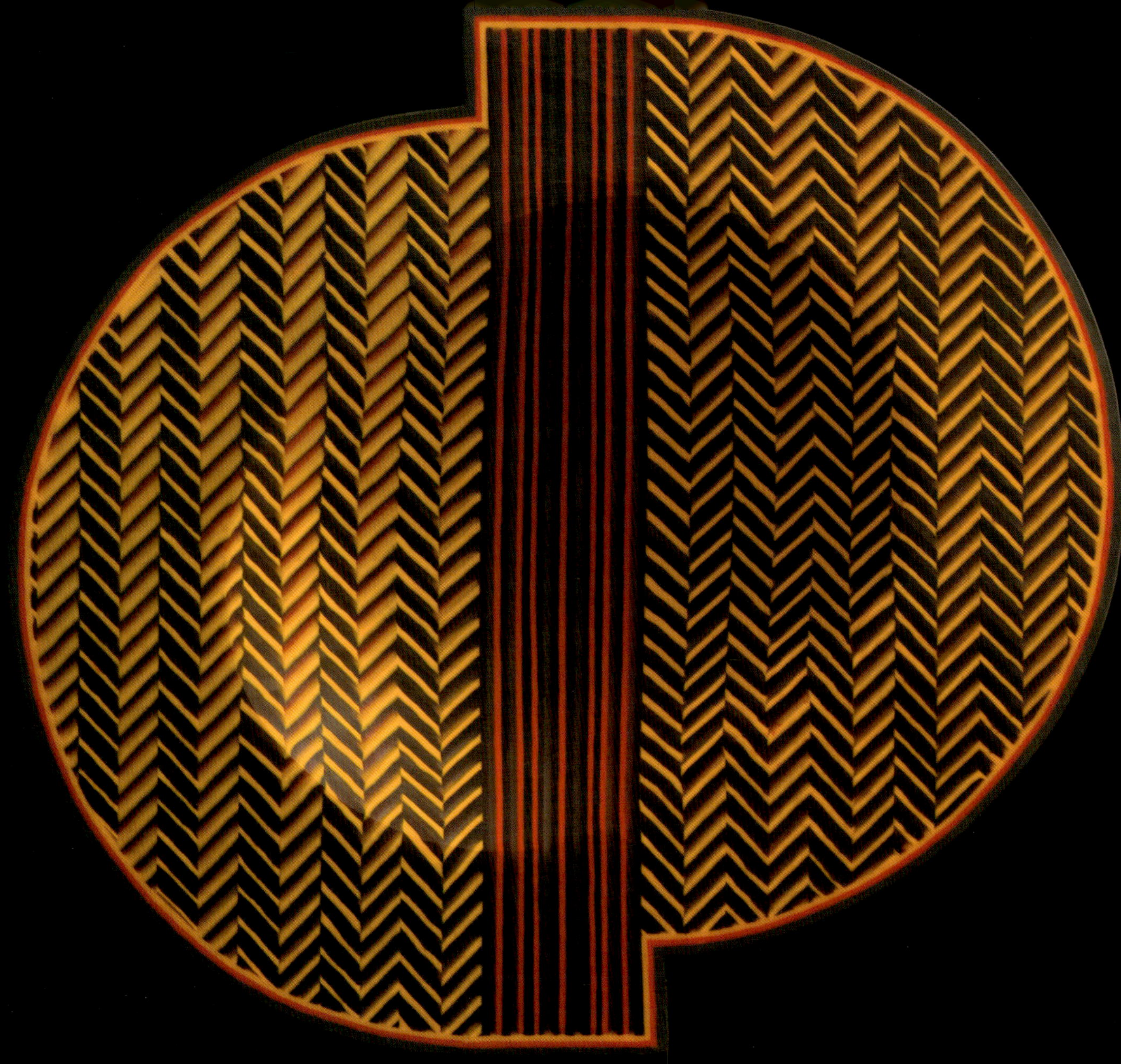

American Connections

Dan Klein

Klaus Moje's life and work have made him an incurable traveller and a citizen of the world. His homeland is Germany, and his destinations have included Australia, his home for the past twenty-six years, and the various countries and towns where he has taught or exhibited. His many visits to the United States have had a profound influence on his career, and also a considerable impact on American glass art. This major exhibition of Moje's work at the Portland Art Museum, drawn largely from public and private U.S. collections, is a tribute to the artist and a recognition of his long involvement with American museums, collectors, educational establishments, and fellow artists.

Klaus Moje first visited the United States in the late 1960s and has exhibited in American galleries since the early 1970s. The Metropolitan Museum of Art in New York was the first museum to acquire a piece by him, in 1979. The piece came from the Heller Gallery and was a joint donation from Doug and Annie Heller and Dale Chihuly.

The work had been solicited by Penelope Hunter-Stiebel, who was curator of twentieth-century decorative arts at the Met. She recalls, "Much as I was shaking my tin cup to build the twentieth-century decorative arts collection, I was extremely selective in the works I wanted. The Met is an encyclopaedic museum, and I believed it should encompass contemporary work, but only in examples that met the standards of the various historic collections."

By 1979 Chihuly and Moje had become good friends, and Chihuly's understanding of Moje's important contribution to the contemporary glass scene resulted in the first of many invitations to Moje to teach at Pilchuck. The emphasis in American glass at the time was on self-expression and the promotion of self, and Chihuly had the kind of foresight that was not common among American artists or aspiring artists in glass. As Tina Oldknow, the curator of modern glass at the Corning Museum of Glass, points out, "In the 1980s, when European artists began to regularly visit to teach in the United States, the most influential I believe were Lino [Tagliapietra], the Libenskys, Bertil [Vallien], and Klaus. The most obvious contribution of the Europeans was technique. But they also contributed knowledge about and experience in making one's way as a

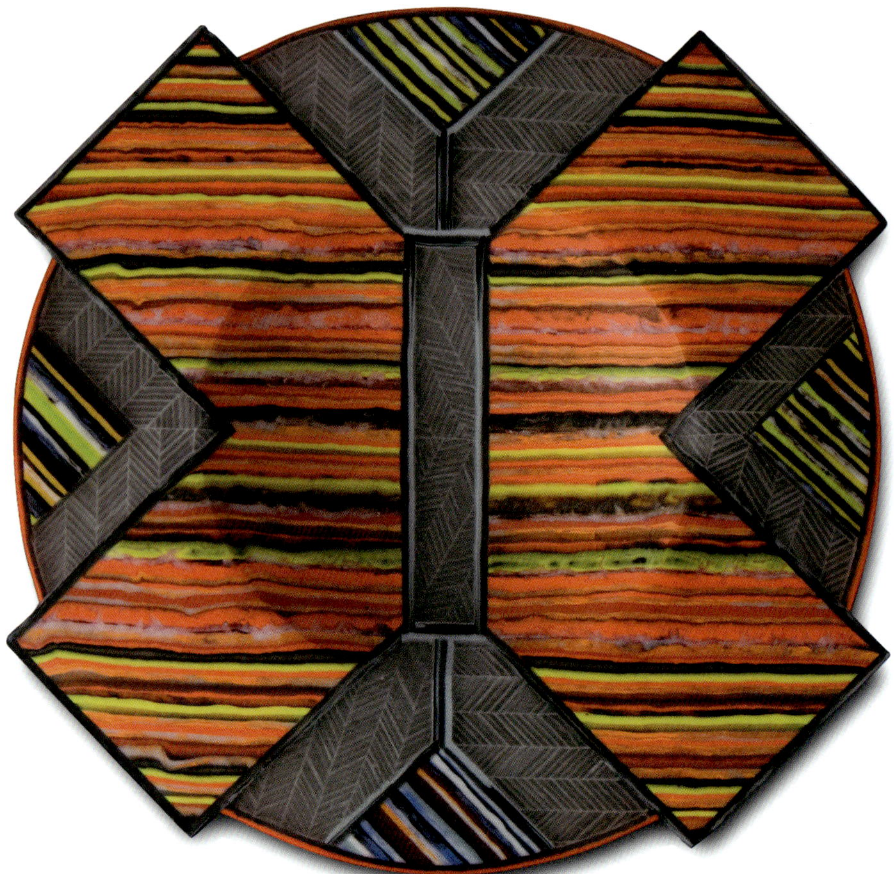

19. Untitled 3, 1986 (#18)

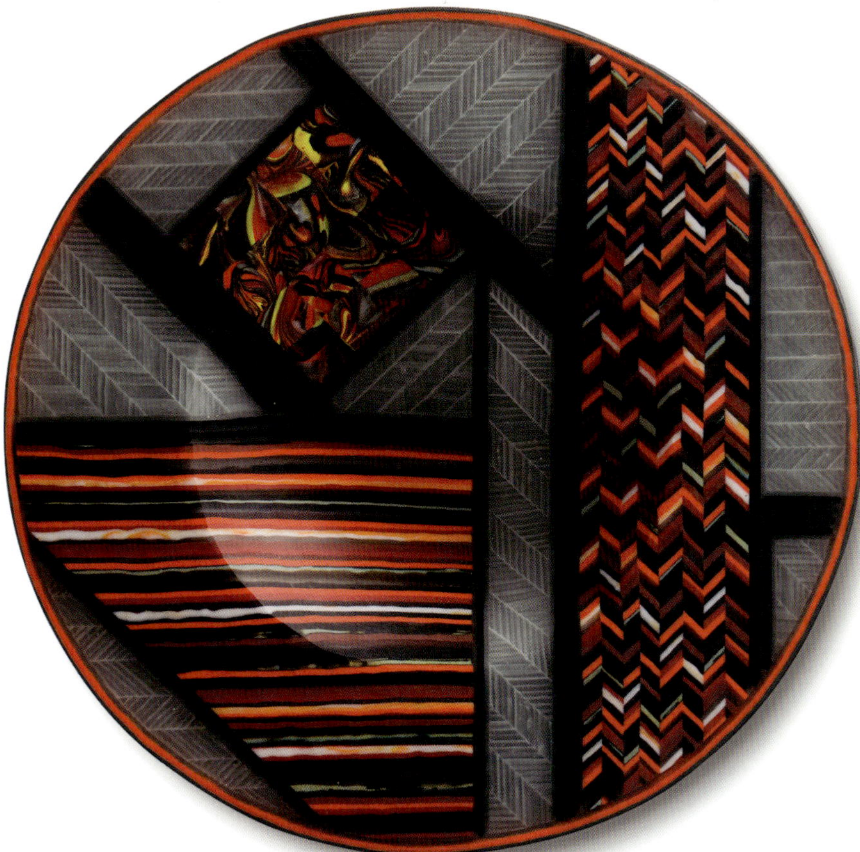

21. Untitled, 1987

professional artist/craftsperson/designer. They brought with them a valuable perspective to studio glass practice. Certainly Klaus was the number one artist in terms of introducing kilnforming techniques to the Americans."

The first session that Klaus Moje taught at Pilchuck is of legendary importance. One of the students in his class, Boyce Lundstrom, realized that Moje offered techniques and artistry that were as yet uncharted, certainly in the United States. Lundstrom, a founding director of Bullseye Glass Company, who later left the company, reported back excitedly to business partner Dan Schwoerer, and a well-documented chapter in the history of modern kilnforming began.

Ted Sawyer, now director of research and education at Bullseye, has been with the company long enough to understand how important Klaus Moje has been to kilnforming and what its techniques now offer artists working in glass in the United States and elsewhere. "It is almost impossible to quantify the tremendous impact that Klaus's approach has had on the American glass scene…He was, of course, one of the major catalysts in the development of Bullseye materials for kiln-glass."

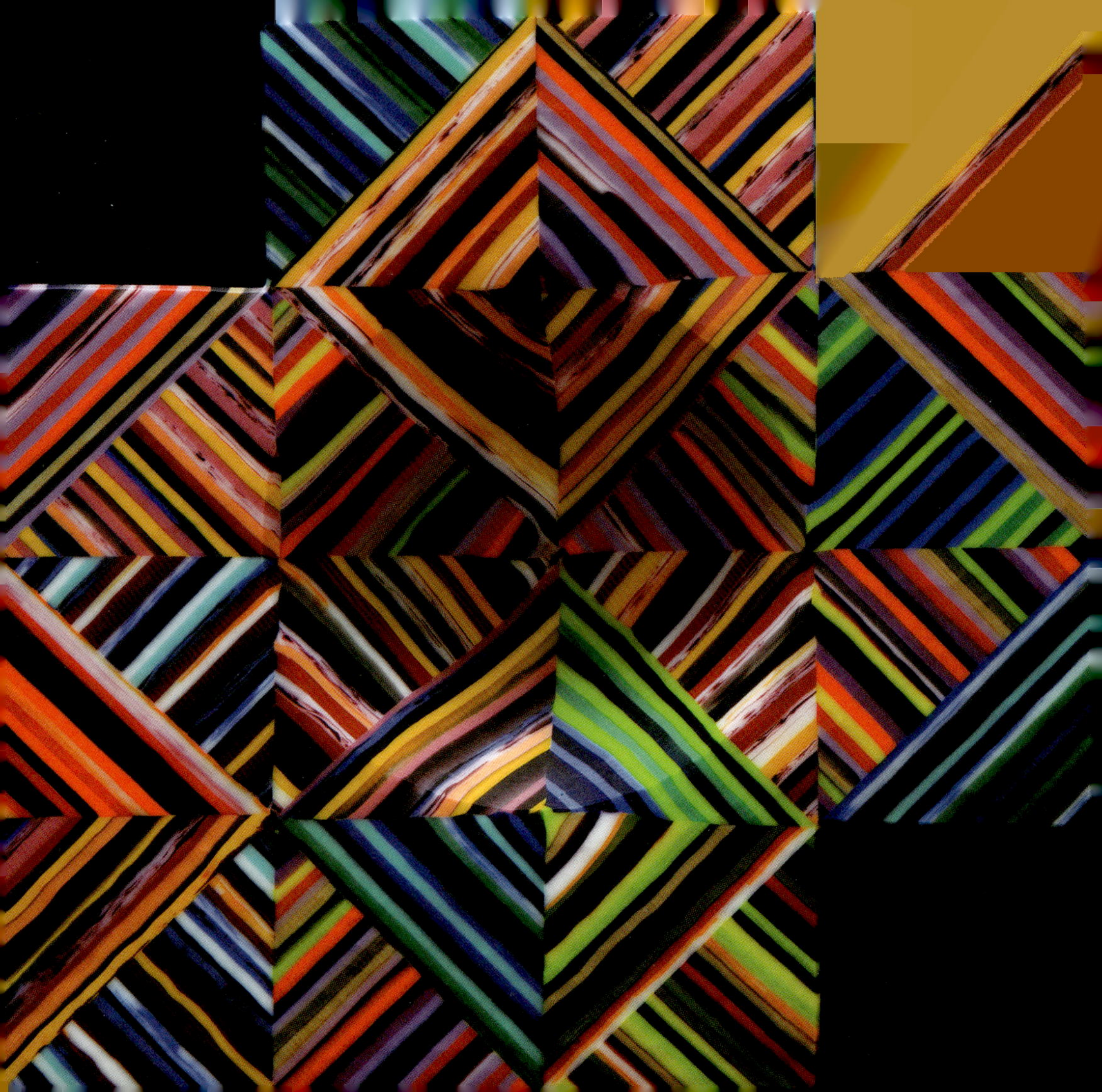

Through Moje's involvement with Pilchuck, Bullseye, and American artists, he developed relationships with many different Americans in the field of education and as an artistic and technical collaborator. One of the most significant of these relationships developed in the work he did with Dante Marioni in 1993. Marioni also feels that Moje "has made a significant contribution to American studio glass, as he essentially pioneered the kilnforming movement." He goes on to say, "Personally, I have always recognized the rather formal training that Klaus had, from an early age, as a driving force in his work, particularly in the early days of studio glass, as there was not a lot of emphasis on being skilled and, moreover, little access to people who were. Klaus brought some thoughtful discipline to a movement that was more about freedom and expression with little knowledge of 'language.'"

Moje spent most of his time from the mid-1980s to the mid-1990s in Canberra to attend to his teaching commitments there. The many talented Australian students who he taught, including Scott Chaseling and Kirstie Rea, have been influential in the United States through exhibitions and their teaching at Pilchuck and other educational establishments. But Moje's methods of working have also directly influenced American education. Dr. John Leighton, who for years has been involved in American glass education at San Francisco State University and California State University, Fullerton, says, "What drew me to Klaus's work, and what set it apart from almost all of the early kilnformed glass that I saw, was his strong design sense and his ability to combine strong color with elegant restraint. There is no doubt in my mind that Klaus had tremendous influence on American glass."

Another admirer from the world of education is Michael Rogers, professor at the School for American Crafts, Rochester Institute of Technology. "Klaus is a true master and mentor. His contribution in an age of 'self-expression' is that an artist must first have a solid technical foundation and a highly developed material sensibility before being able to successfully communicate through visual arts. Klaus had and has a methodical approach to developing ideas in glass, and in terms of education, this has had a significant effect internationally." Marvin Lipofksy, founder of the glass program at the California College of Arts and Crafts, simply adds, "What was really important was his winning personality. He is very intelligent."

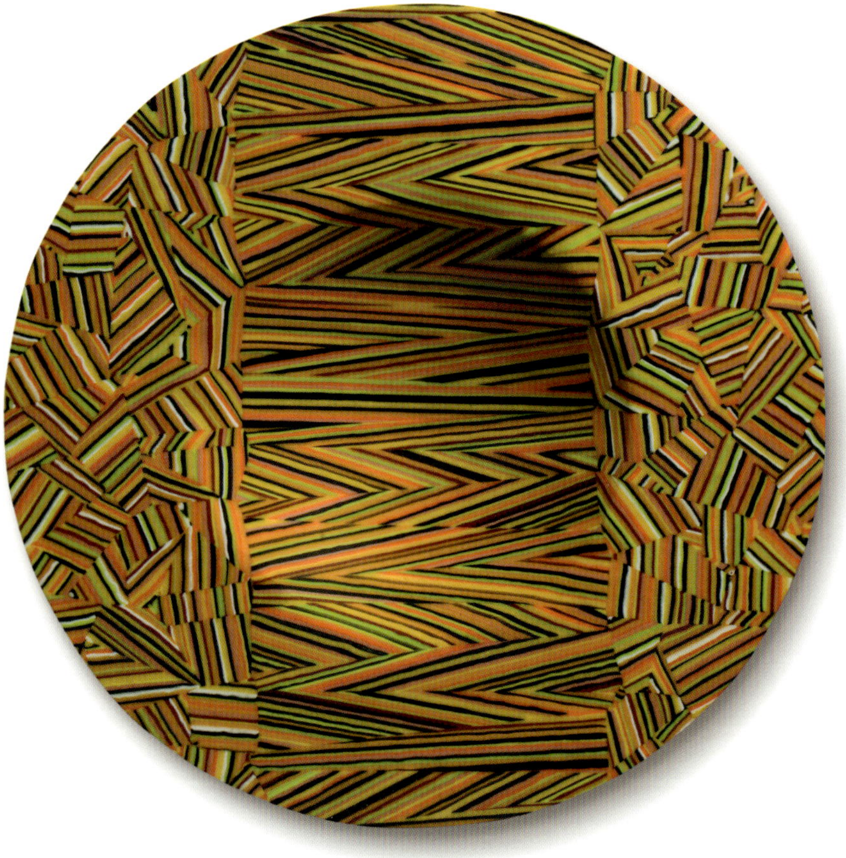

55. Untitled 10, 2006

Making art has always been at the heart of Klaus Moje's activities. Even as a mentor he follows a way of teaching that leads by example—not by encouraging imitation, but by demonstrating that there are no shortcuts to hours of work and hard-earned skill. These are the qualities that have earned him his reputation as one of the world's most significant artists in glass. Tina Oldknow at Corning says, "I consider Klaus to be one of the very important pioneering generation of European glass artists."

His work is in many American museum collections, including the Metropolitan Museum and the Museum of Arts and Design in New York, Palm Springs Art Museum, San Francisco's de Young Museum, Toledo Museum of Art, and the Corning Museum of Glass. He also has a strong following among a handful of major American collectors. Quite a few of them, like Henry Hillman Jr. and Harold and Arlene Schnitzer, are based in Portland. They, like all collectors of his work it seems, collect it in depth.

The present exhibition bears witness to the long-term commitment of some of these collectors, such as George and Dorothy Saxe from the San Francisco area, and Dan Greenberg and Susan Steinhauser from Los Angeles. Thanks to their generosity, San Francisco's de Young Museum and the Los Angeles County Museum of Art have important holdings of Moje's work. Cynthia and Jeffrey Manocherian discovered Moje's work on a trip through Germany, before it began being sold in the United States. By the mid-1980s they were buying his pieces wherever they could, from the Heller Gallery in New York, from Habatat in Detroit and Florida, from Ruth Summers in Los Angeles, from Siegfried Ehrman's Compositions Gallery in San Francisco, and from the Glass Art Gallery in Toronto.

Of these only Habatat and Heller still exist, and they have shown the artist's work consistently for nearly thirty years. It never fails to sell to the handful of American collectors who have, in a sense, become addicted to it. His ordered palette is not typically American, and as Doug Heller indicates, Moje's work stands out in an American gallery: "What I saw in Klaus was a mature and highly accomplished artist creating work unlike any other the gallery represented." Ferdinand Hampson of Habatat adds, "I first met Klaus in 1979 at the Corning New Glass exhibition. He had a couple of pieces with him, and we consigned them. I had seen his work in a couple of publications prior to this. I believe that Klaus has had an impact in what has occurred in the U.S.

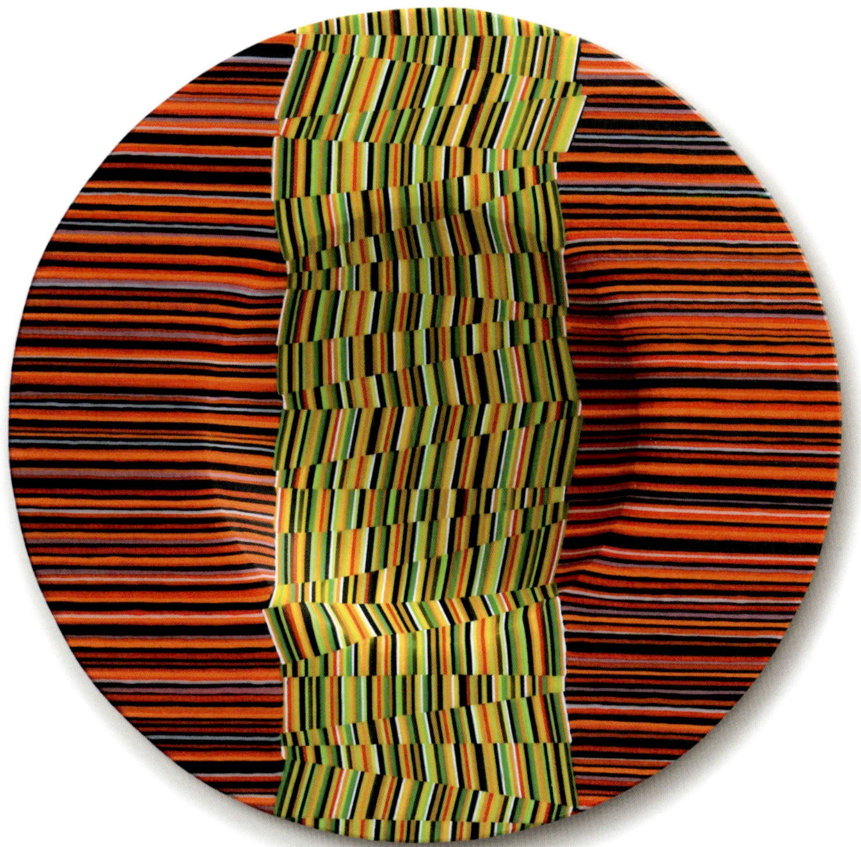

49. Untitled, 2003–05 (from the *Impact Series*)

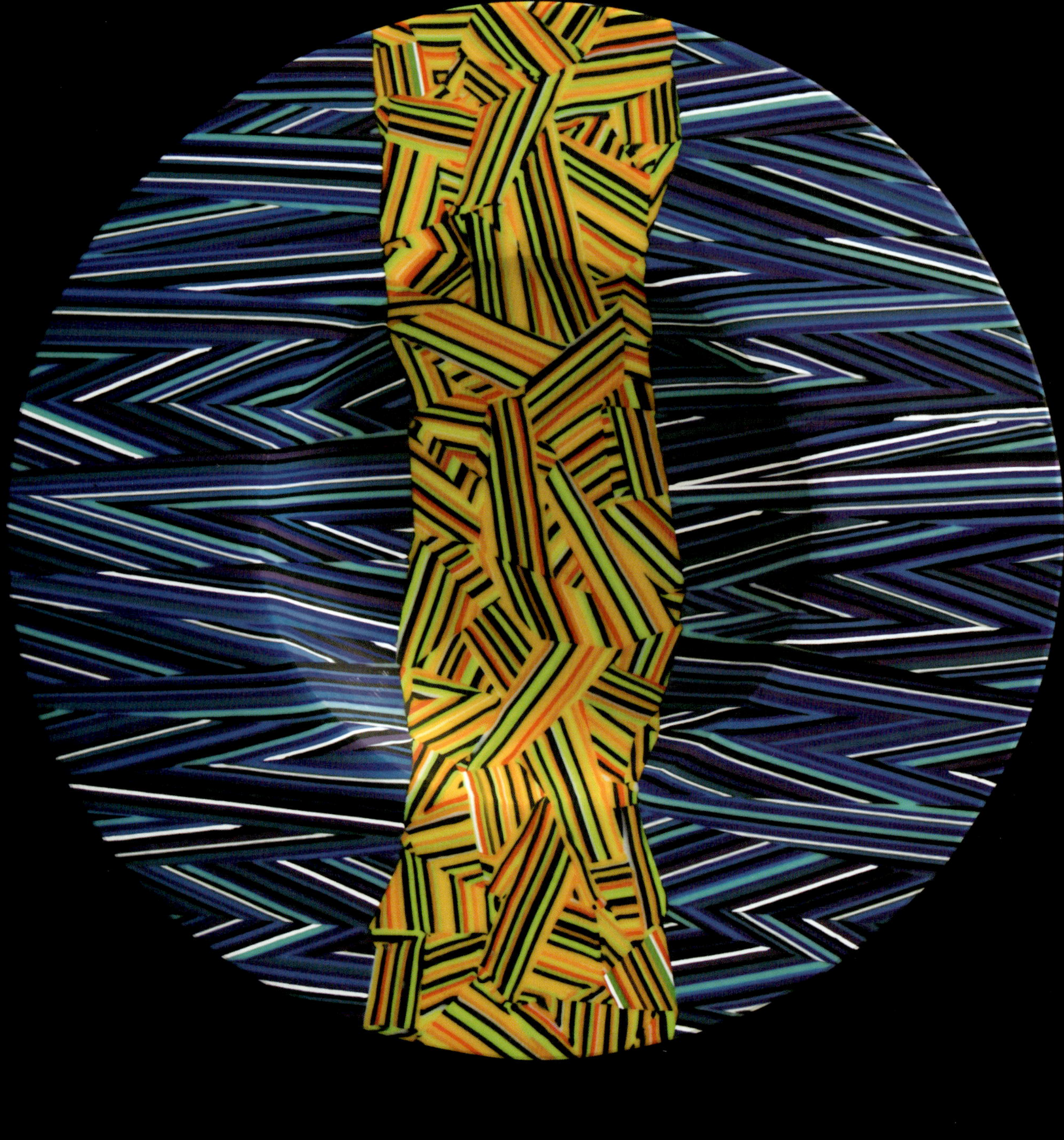

48. Untitled, 2003–05 (from the *Impact Series*)

Certainly his experiments in the early 1980s with Bullseye Glass, that ultimately resulted in being able to fuse more than three colors together, had an impact. The first series, called 'New Horizon,' created quite a stir."

Dan Schwoerer and Lani McGregor's special working relationship with Klaus Moje at Bullseye Glass has given them perhaps the most significant insight into his way of working. Lani McGregor sums up her thoughts about their collaboration by saying very simply, "Klaus the relentlessly original visual explorer has come to signify for us what *can* be at the heart even of a manufacturing operation. Without the soul of the artist, what are any of us doing here?" ■

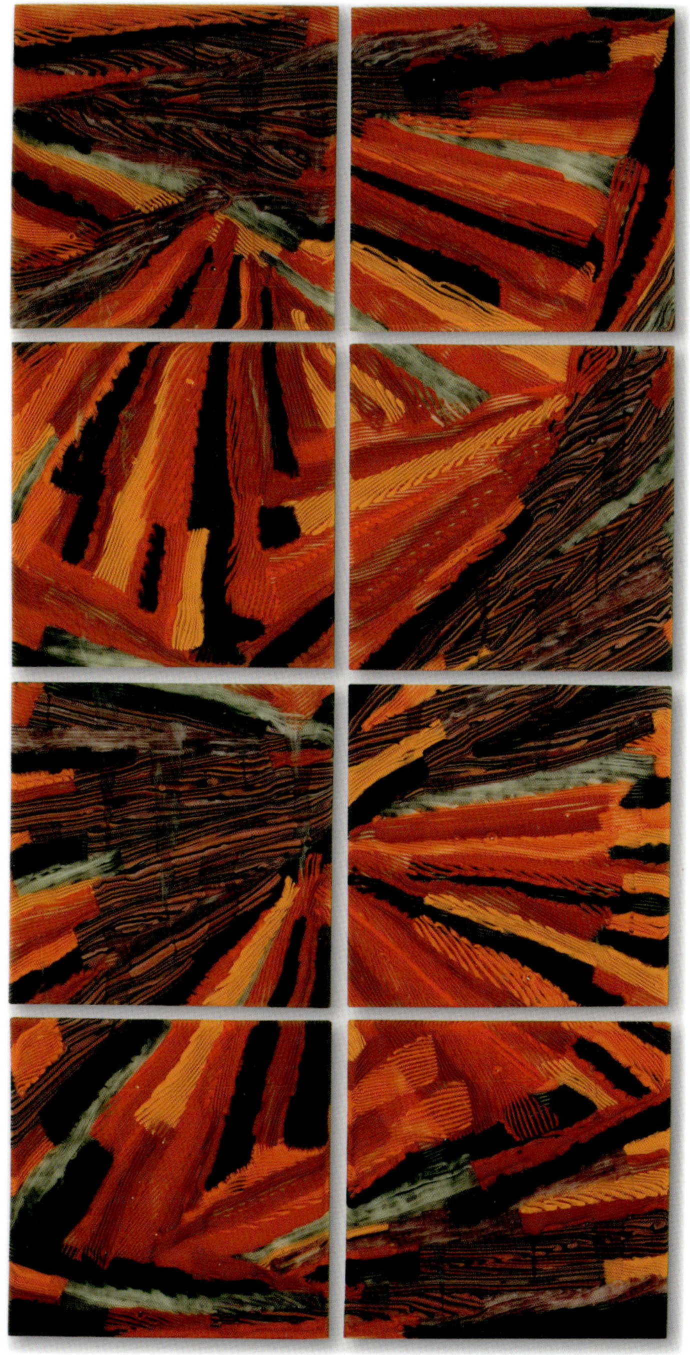

64. Untitled 10, 2006

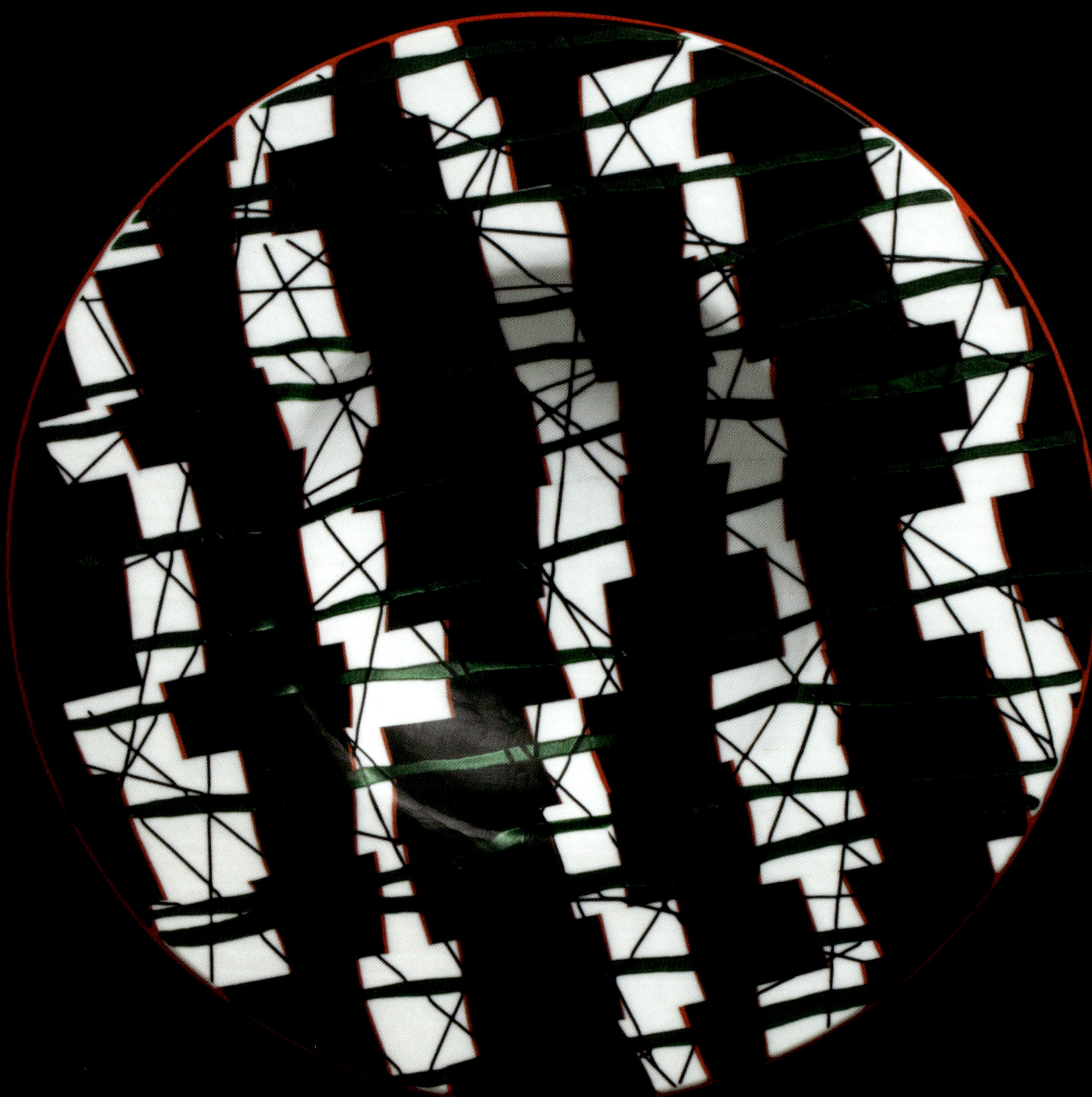

57. Untitled 9, 2006

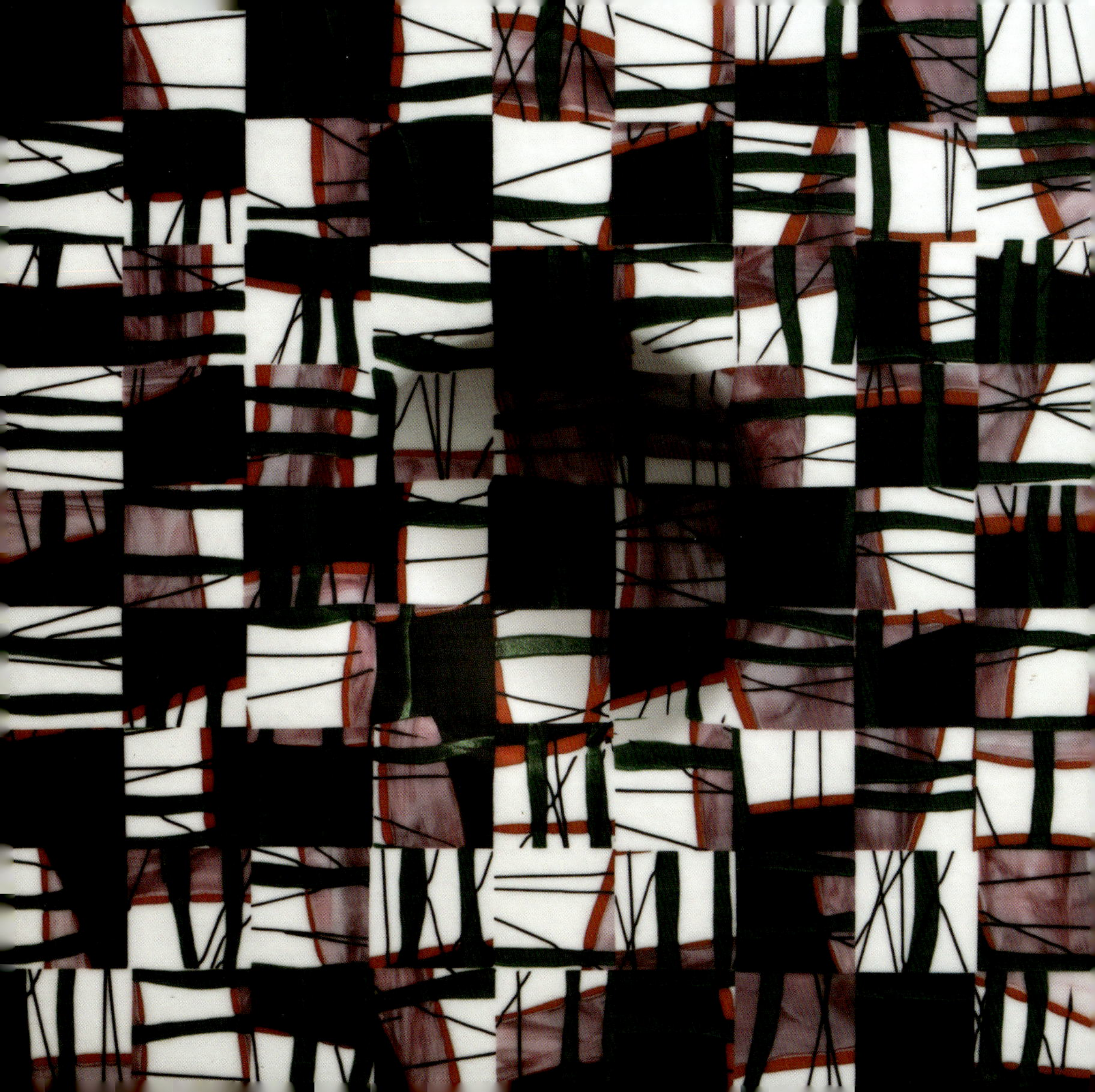

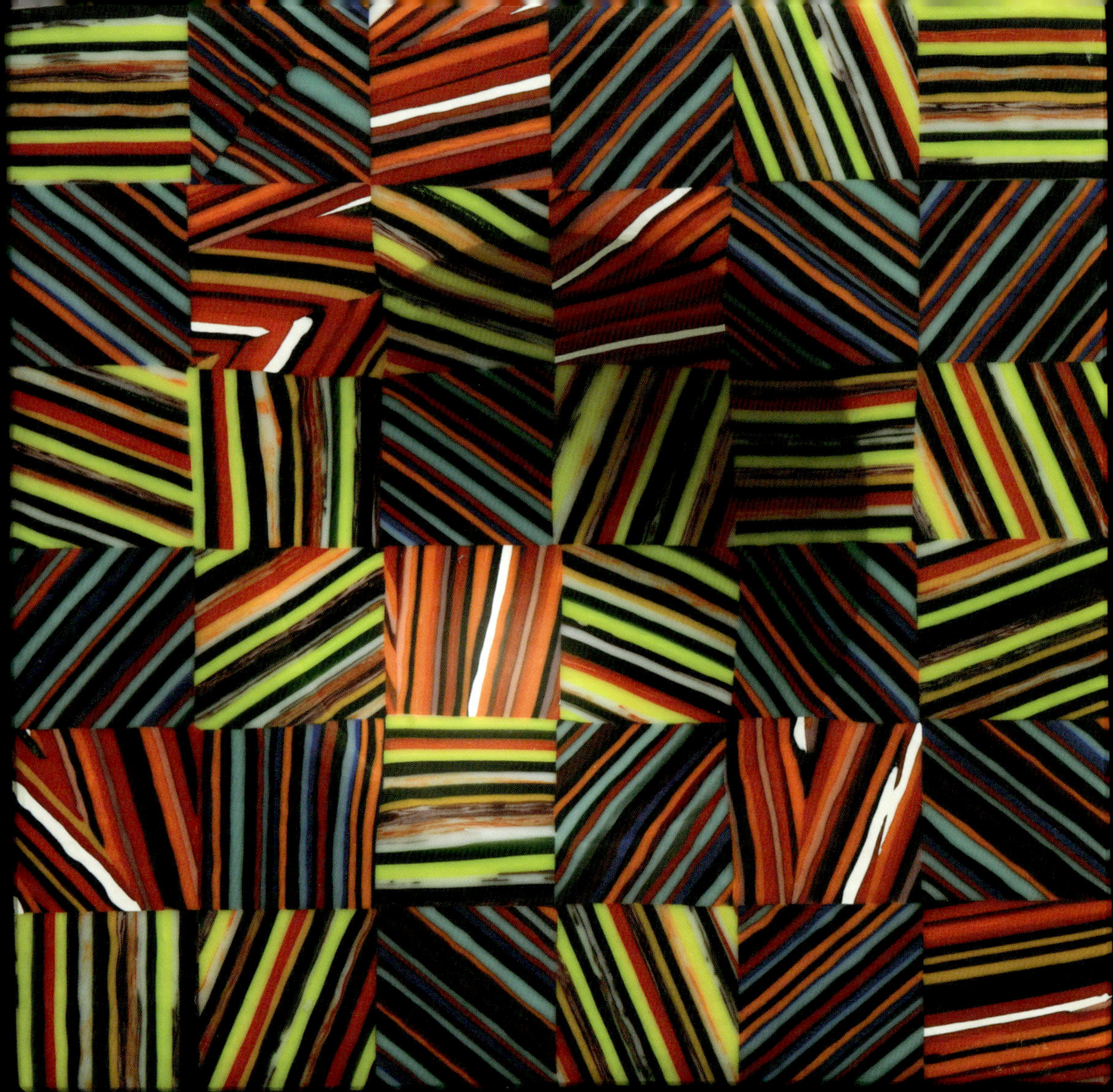

62. Untitled 11, 2006

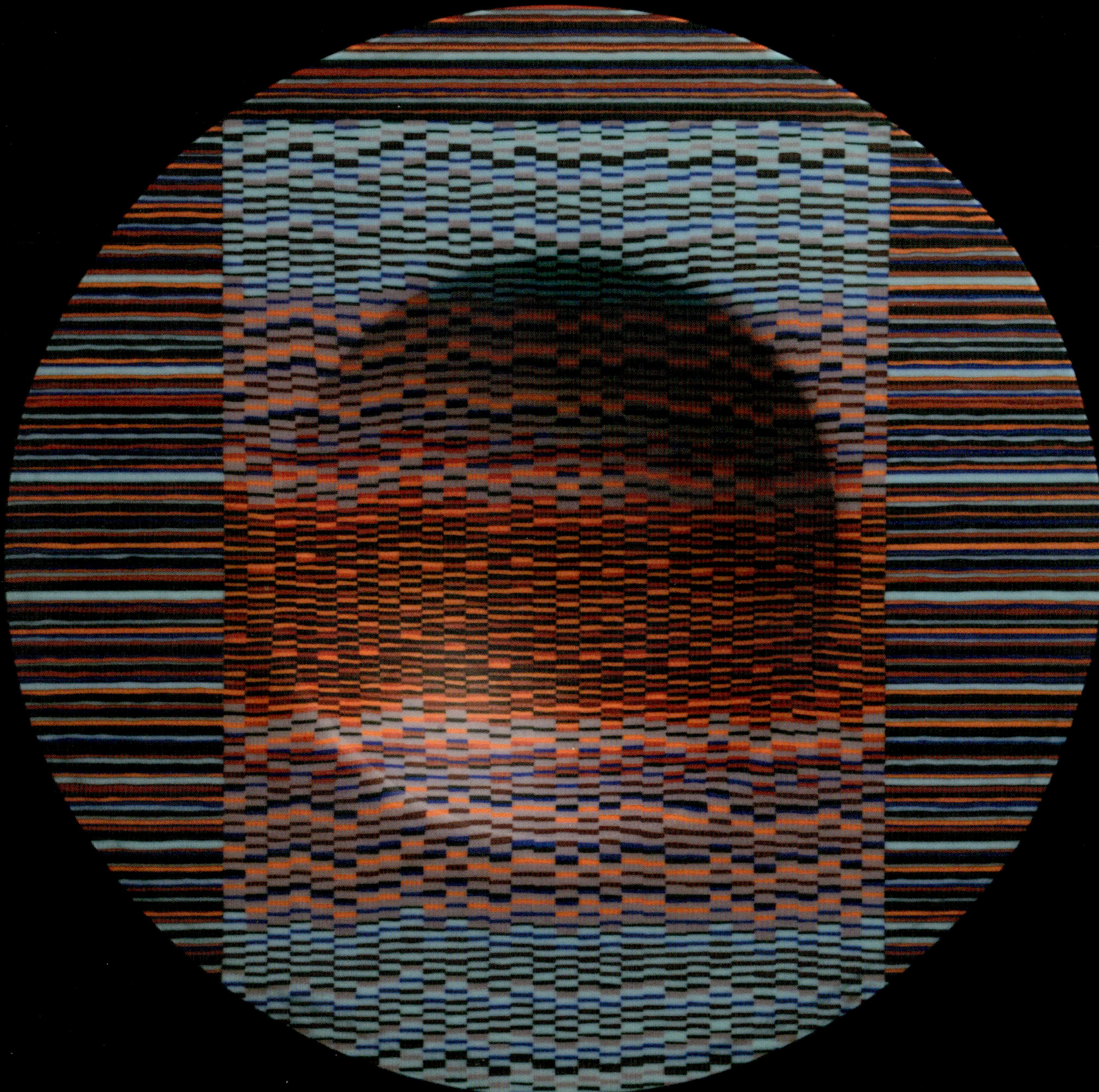

59. Untitled 6, 2006

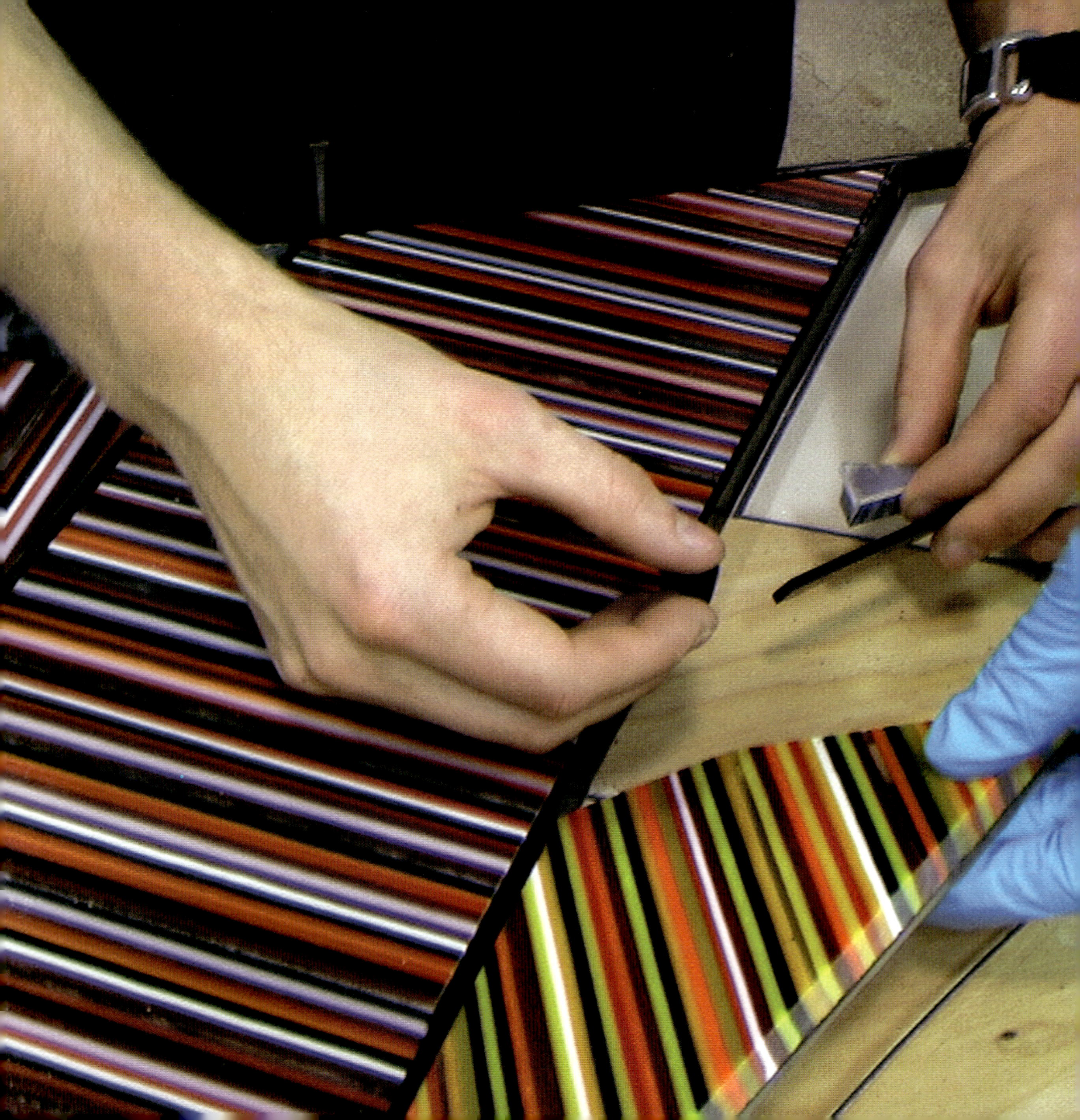

A Technical Perspective on The Portland Panels

Ted Sawyer

In April 2007, Klaus Moje visited the Research and Education studio at the Bullseye Glass factory in Portland, Oregon, with ambitious plans to make four intricately patterned fused-glass panels, each measuring 6 feet by 4 feet by 5/8 inches. Panels of this size would be the largest that he had ever composed and executed. To bring them to completion would require the artist to work almost entirely alone for a long period of time or to work with a skilled team of assistants, which would facilitate the realization of the artist's vision more rapidly. Completing the panels would also require a kiln much larger than the one the artist had in his studio in Australia.

Moje returned to Australia to develop the work through a series of drawings and experiments. He then instructed the team at Bullseye to begin making the basic components that he would work with after he returned to Portland. These patterned components were 19-by-19-by-3/8-inch

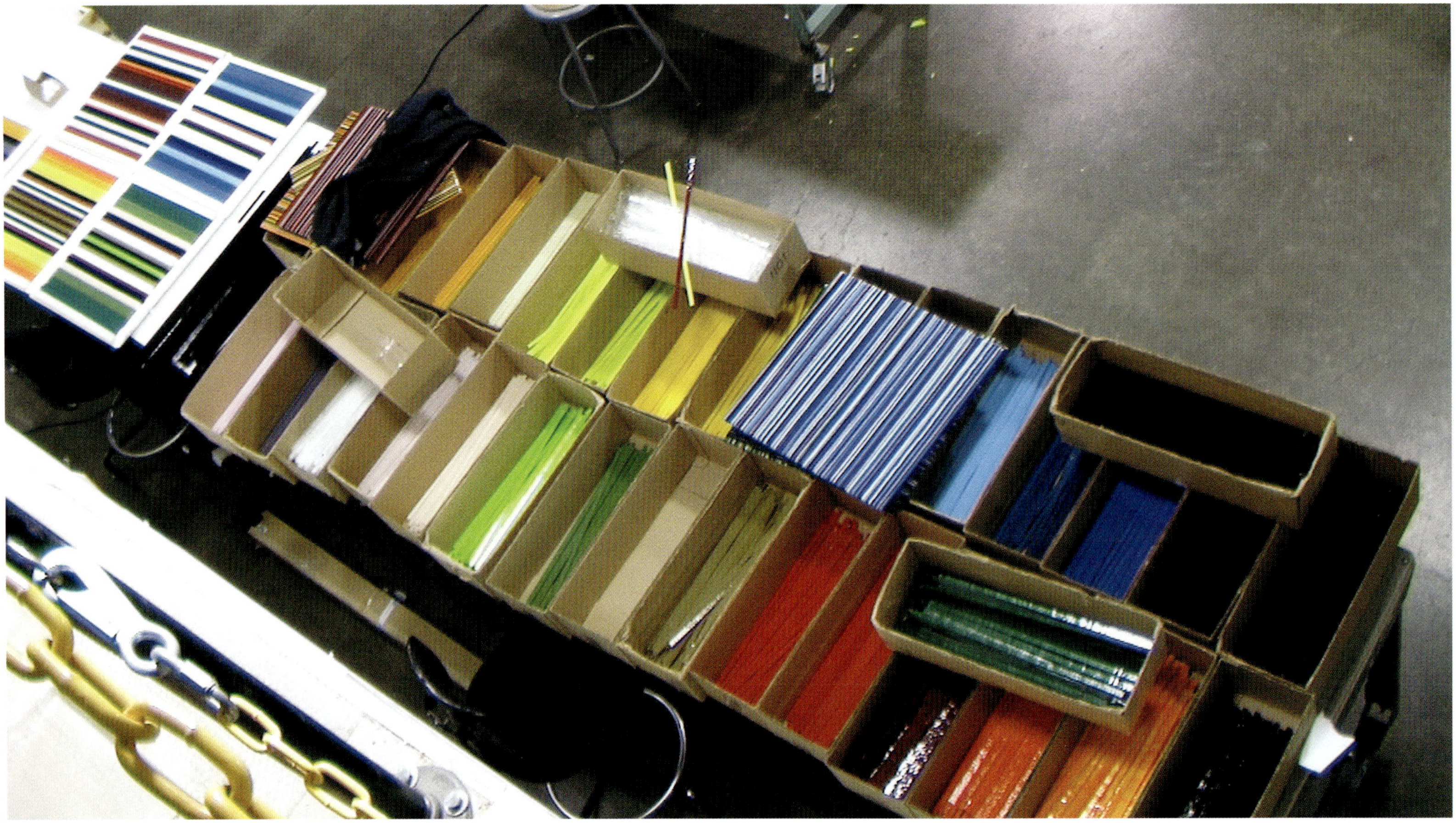

Palette of handcut strips of glass and test panels in the Bullseye glass studio.

panels made from 1/8-inch strips of clear and colored transparent and opalescent glasses. The panels were fused by heating them in a kiln to a temperature of 1,540°F and then carefully cooling them. By the end of the project, the team had hand cut over twenty-two thousand strips of sheet glass 19 by 3/8 by 1/8 inches to make over one hundred such panels. Although not all the strips that were cut or the components that were made ended up in the finished works, having these materials available was important to the artist as he brought the works to their final resolution.

When Moje returned to Bullseye in June of 2007, he began to oversee production of the components that remained to be made, making many decisions about palette and pattern as the larger works evolved. At the same time he began to cut these panels into specific shapes that would ultimately fit together. To precisely cut this thick,

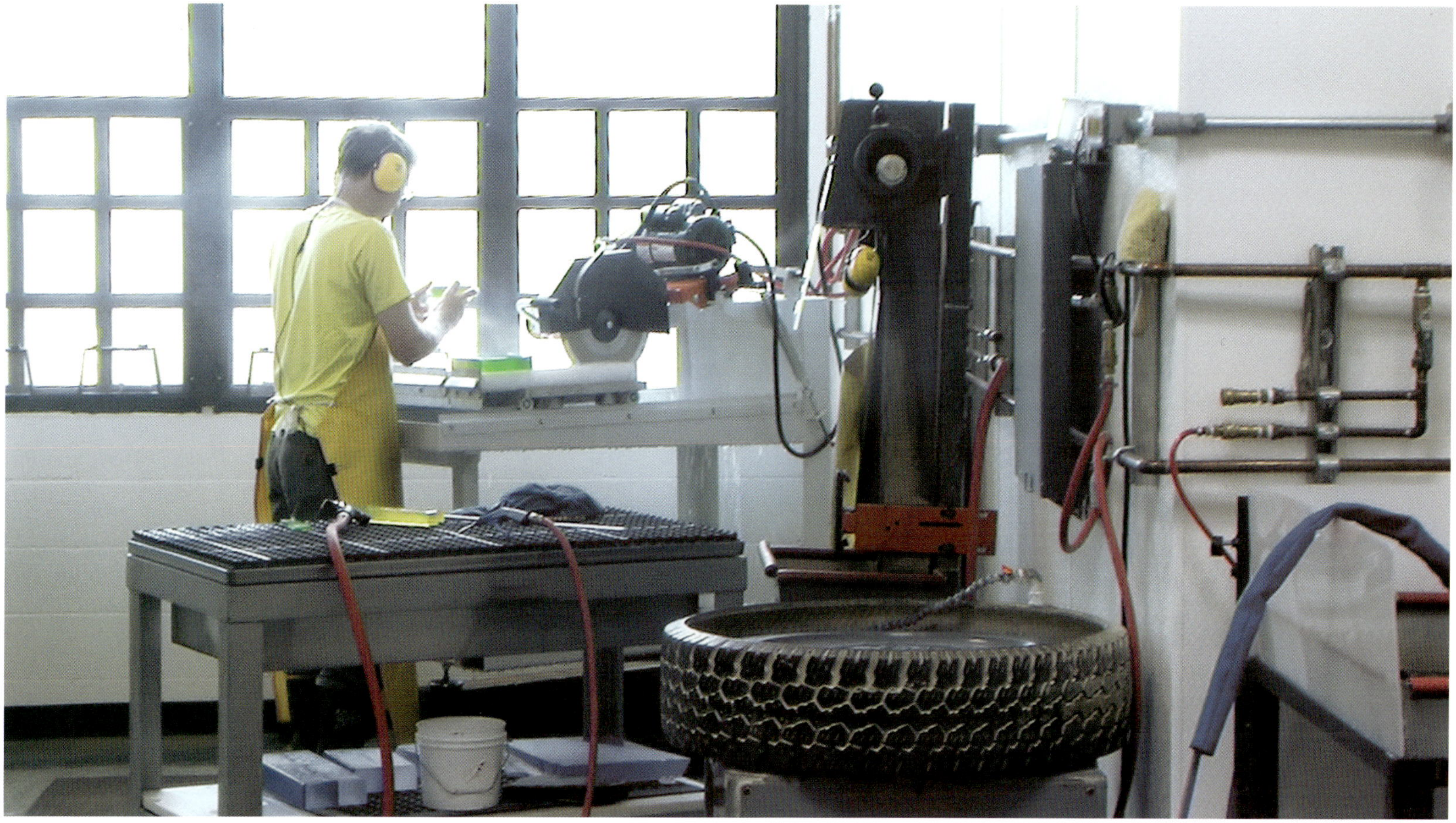

Diamond-sawing fused elements for The Portland Panels.

prefused glass he used a water-cooled saw with a diamond-impregnated blade.

As he cut the components necessary for a given panel, he began to assemble them in layers on a large horizontal surface made of plywood, everything held in place with horseshoe nails, as is often done in the composition of stained-glass works. While he was working, an assistant followed behind him and hand cut pieces of sheet

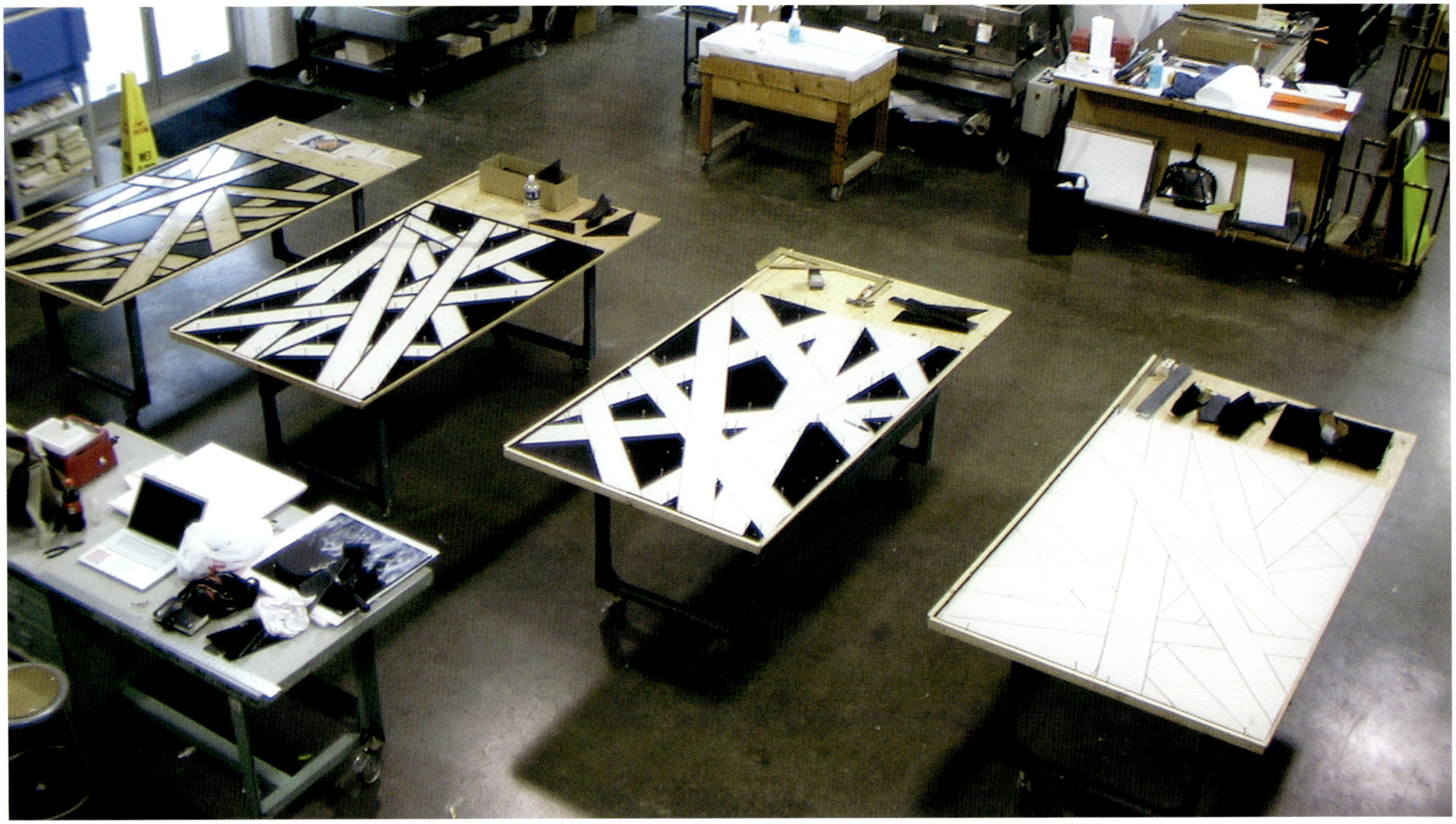

The Portland Panels in progress on plywood background matrix.

glass that matched the cuts that Moje had made on the saw to elevate some components and to put a light gauze of blended clear and white glass over others.

Once assembled, the entire panel was painstakingly transferred to another horizontal surface, this one an 11-by-5-foot, high-temperature shelf inside a kiln. Once the panel was on the shelf, dams of high-temperature ceramic fiberboard were placed around the piece to keep it from flowing outward when heated. The kiln was closed, slowly fired to a temperature of 1,540°F, and then cooled over the course of three days.

Coming out of the kiln, the top surface of glass was extremely glossy. This surface was ideal for unloading the works, which weighed almost two hundred pounds, by using large suction cups and a team of people. The glossy surface was not,

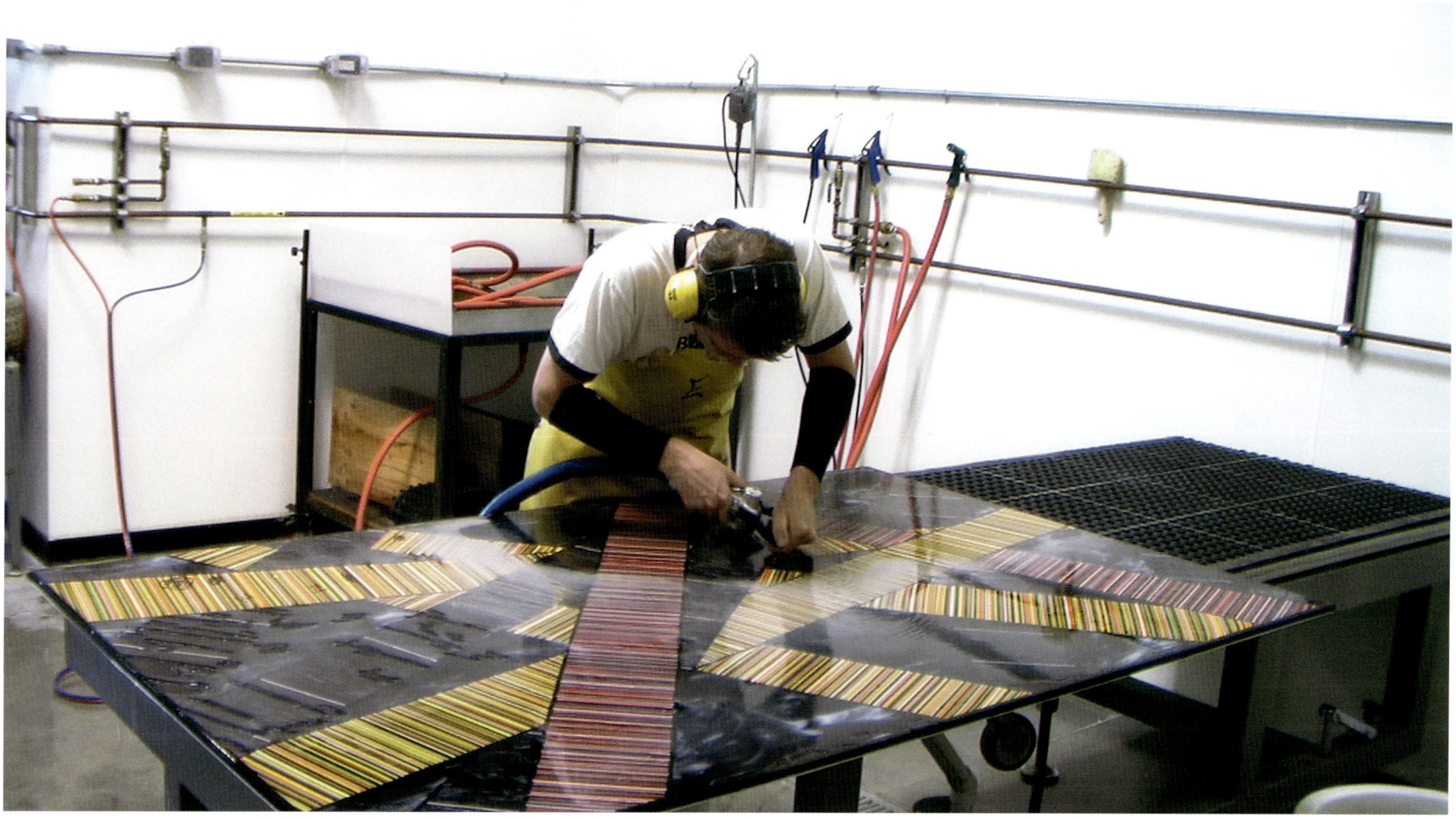

Grinding the surface of finished panels to create a matte honed finish.

87

however, ideally suited to Moje's aesthetics. It was critical to him that this shiny surface, with its attendant glare that makes it difficult to see into the glass, be removed. As such, each panel was ground down using diamond pads on a hand-held, water-fed pneumatic angle grinder to give it a honed finish.

Finally, a special hanging system was developed for the works. The system uses two metal cleats

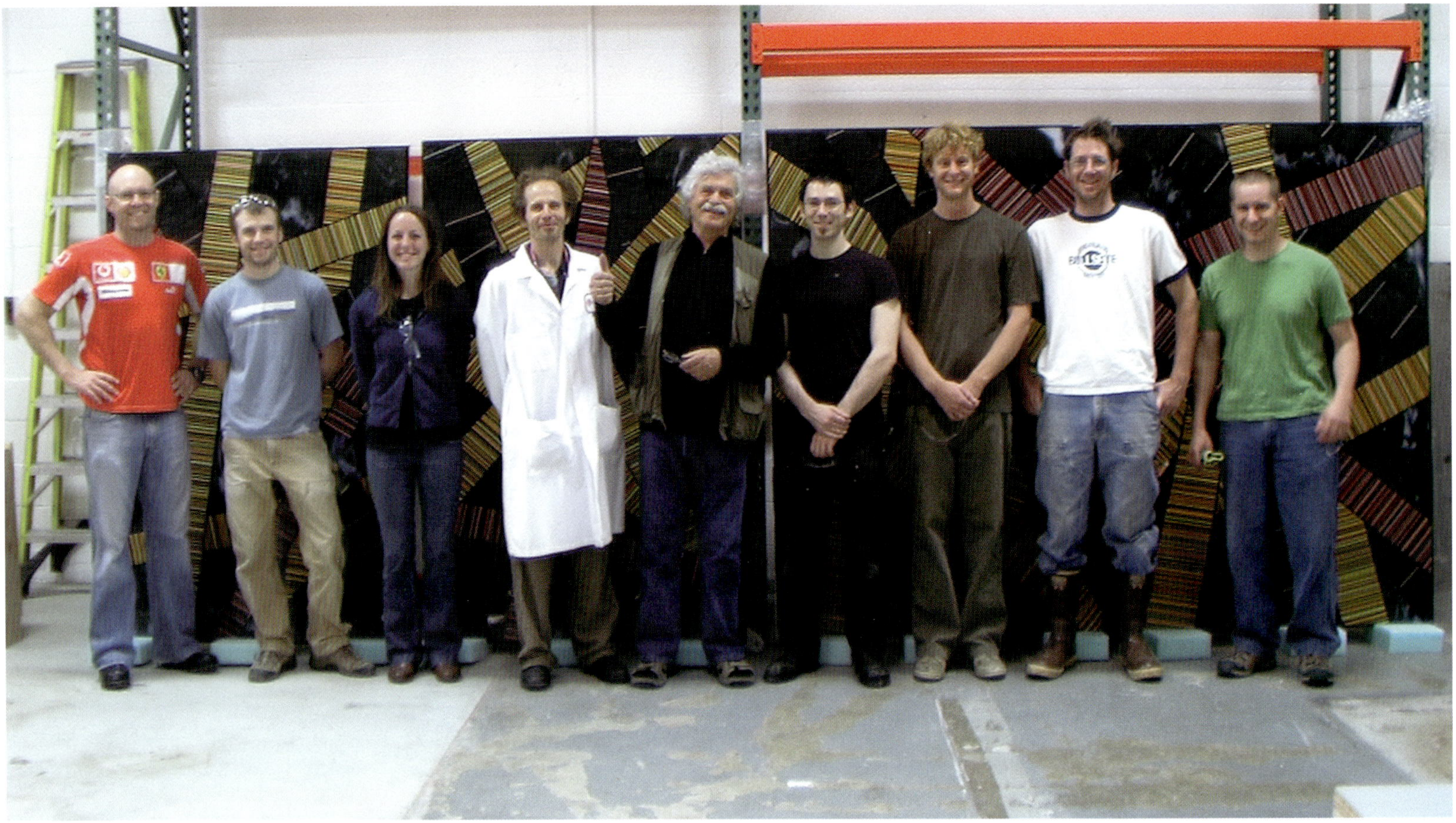

Left to right: Mark Picard, Tom Jacobs, Jaclyn Kampmeier, Ted Sawyer, Klaus Moje, Louis Delegato, Nathan Sandberg, Erik Whittemore and Paul McNulty.

that are adhered to the backs of the pieces by using an architectural grade silicone that has been tested to hold fifty times the weight required. These cleats interlock with another set of cleats that are fastened to a 1-inch white board. The advantage of this system is that the board can be safely and precisely mounted to a standard wall, and when the glass panel is hung on the cleats it will be level and secure.

In all a team of nine people had a role in assisting Moje or working on other aspects of this project, logging over six hundred hours. Moje himself seemed to be at the studio around the clock for the five weeks that he was in Portland. ■

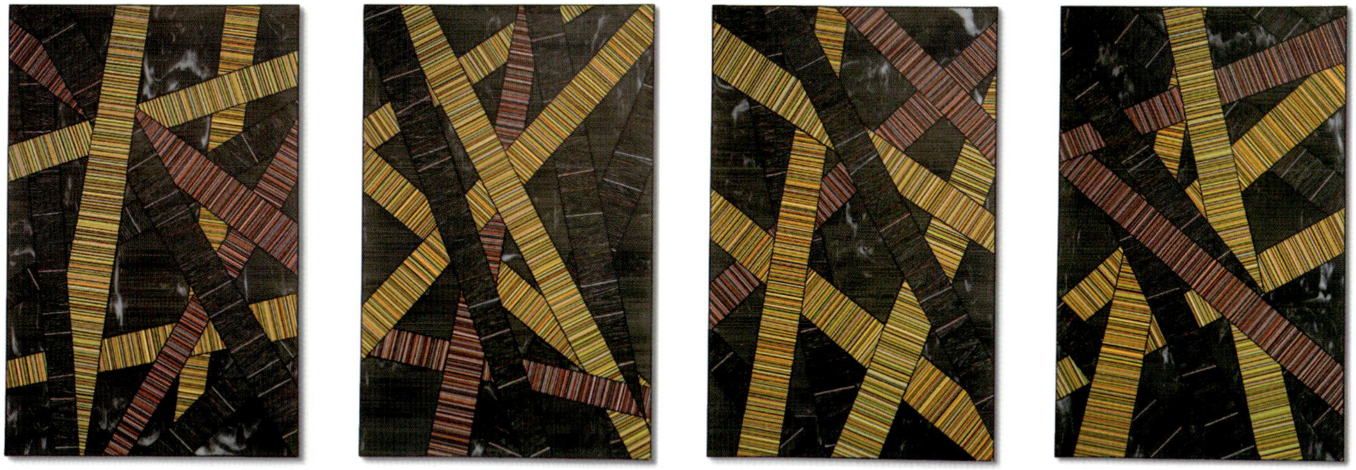

67. The Portland Panels: Choreographed Geometry, 2007

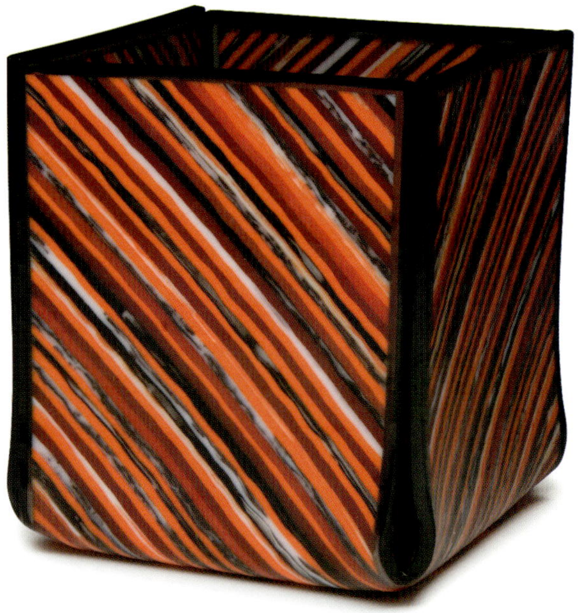

31. Untitled 8, 1993

Checklist

1. **Carved Vessel, c. 1976**
Blown lead glass, cut
3¼ x 3⅞ inches diameter (8.2 x 9.9 cm)
The Corning Museum of Glass;
Gift of Klaus Moje

2. **Untitled Cut Crystal, late 1970s**
Blown lead glass, cut, iridized, and refired
2¾ x 4¾ inches diameter (7 x 12 cm)
Anonymous lender, New York

3. **Untitled Cut Crystal, late 1970s**
Blown lead glass, cut
8 x 2¼ x 2¼ inches (20.3 x 5.5 x 5.5 cm)
Private collection, New York

4. **Untitled 5, 1977**
Rods of glass, sliced, kilnformed, and wheel cut
8¾ x 6 x 1⅝ inches (22.3 x 15.3 x 4.2 cm)
Collection of Daniel Greenberg and
Susan Steinhauser, Los Angeles

5. **Mosaic Glass Bowl, 1977**
Rods of glass, stripped, kilnformed, and wheel cut
2¼ x 12 inches diameter (5.7 x 30.7 cm)
The Corning Museum of Glass

6. **Untitled, 1977-78**
Rods of glass, stripped, kilnformed, and wheel cut
2¾ x 7½ inches diameter (7 x 19 cm)
Anonymous lender, New York

7. **Untitled, 1978**
Rods of glass, stripped, kilnformed, and wheel cut
3 x 18½ inches diameter (7.5 x 47.2 cm)
Collection of Ruth T. Summers and
Bruce W. Bowen, Asheville, North Carolina

8. **Yellow Bowl Oval, 1979**
Rods of glass, sliced, kilnformed, and wheel cut
10¼ x 7⅞ x 2⅛ inches (26 x 20 x 5.5 cm)
Collection of Brigitte Enders, Canberra, Australia

9. **Untitled Bowl (Lifesaver), 1979**
Rods of glass, sliced, kilnformed, and wheel cut
3⅞ x 10⅛ inches diameter (8 x 25.5 cm)
Toledo Museum of Art;
Gift of Dorothy and George Saxe

10. **Untitled, 1980**
Rods of glass, stripped, kilnformed, and wheel cut
12¾ x 9¾ x 2¾ (32.4 x 24.8 x 7.1 cm)
The Corning Museum of Glass

11. **Untitled, 1981**
Rods of glass, stripped, kilnformed, and wheel cut
10 x 13½ x 2¾ inches (25.4 x 34.3 x 7 cm)
Private collection, New York

12. **Untitled, 1981**
Rods of glass, stripped, kilnformed, and wheel cut
2 x 11⅛ inches diameter (5 x 28 cm)
Anonymous lender, New York

13. **Untitled, c. 1982**
Rods of glass, sliced, kilnformed, and wheel cut
10 x 13 x 2¾ inches (25.4 x 33 x 7 cm)
Private collection, New York

14. **Untitled 5, 1982**
Rods of glass, sliced, kilnformed, and wheel cut
12 x 11 x 2¼ inches (30.5 x 28 x 5.7 cm)
Anonymous lender, New York

15. **Untitled 11, 1983 (#18)**
Rods of glass, stripped, kilnformed, and wheel cut
20 x 21 x 3 inches (50.8 x 53.3 x 7.6 cm)
Los Angeles County Museum of Art

16. **Untitled 9, 1984** (from the ***New Horizon Series***)
Sheet glass, stripped, kilnformed, and wheel cut
16¾ x 16¾ x 2 inches (42.5 x 42.5 x 5 cm)
Private collection, New York

17. **Untitled, 1985**
Rods of glass, stripped, kilnformed, and wheel cut
21¼ x 22½ x 2½ inches (53.3 x 55.9 x 5.5 cm)
Anonymous lender, New York

18. **Untitled, 1986**
Rods of glass, sliced, kilnformed, and wheel cut
3¼ x 18¼ inches diameter (8.2 x 46.4 cm)
Private collection, New York

19. **Untitled 3, 1986 (#18)**
Sheet glass, stripped, kilnformed, and wheel cut
2 x 20¼ inches diameter (5 x 51.4 cm)
Collection of Daniel Greenberg and
Susan Steinhauser, Los Angeles

20. **Untitled 1, 1986 (#3)**
Rods of glass, stripped, kilnformed, and wheel cut
2½ x 18½ inches diameter (5.5 x 47.3 cm)
Anonymous lender, New York

21. **Untitled, 1987**
Sheet glass, stripped, kilnformed, and wheel cut
2½ x 19¾ inches diameter (6.4 x 50.2 cm)
Private collection, New York

22. **Untitled, 1987 (#24)**
Sheet glass, stripped, kilnformed, and wheel cut
2¼ x 13⅝ x 18½ inches (5.5 x 34.7 x 46 cm)
Anonymous lender, New York

23. **Untitled 3, 1989**
Sheet glass, stripped, kilnformed, and wheel cut
3 x 19 inches diameter (7.5 x 48.3 cm)
Collection of Arlene and Harold Schnitzer,
Portland, Oregon

24. **Songlines, 1989**
Sheet glass, stripped, kilnformed, and wheel cut
19 x 19 x 3 inches (48.3 x 48.3 x 7.5 cm)
Collection of Arlene and Harold Schnitzer,
Portland, Oregon

25. **Untitled, 1989**
Sheet glass, stripped, kilnformed, and wheel cut
3 x 21 inches diameter (7.5 x 53 cm)
Private collection, New York

26. **Untitled, 1989**
Sheet glass, stripped, kilnformed, and wheel cut
17 x 17 x 2 inches (43.2 x 43.2 x 5 cm)
Collection of Dorothy and George Saxe,
San Francisco

27. **Untitled 1, 1990 (#2)**
Sheet glass, stripped, kilnformed, and wheel cut
3 x 20⅛ inches diameter (7.5 x 51 cm)
Collection of Arlene and Harold Schnitzer,
Portland, Oregon

28. **Untitled 2, 1990 (#9)**
Glass rod, sliced, stripped, kilnformed, and
wheel cut
2 x 13 inches diameter (5.1 x 33 cm)
Collection of Daniel Greenberg and
Susan Steinhauser, Los Angeles

29. **Untitled 7, 1990 (#31)**
Sheet glass, stripped, kilnformed, and wheel cut
17 x 18 x 2½ inches (43.2 x 45.7 x 6.4 cm)
Collection of Daniel Greenberg and
Susan Steinhauser, Los Angeles

30. **Untitled, 1991 (#19)**
Sheet glass, stripped, kilnformed, and wheel cut
2⅜ x 21¼ inches diameter (6 x 54 cm)
Collection of Daniel Schwoerer and
Lani McGregor, Portland, Oregon

31. **Untitled 8, 1993**
Sheet glass, stripped, kilnformed, and wheel cut
7 x 6 x 6 inches (17.8 x 15.2 x 15.2 cm)
Collection of Arlene and Harold Schnitzer,
Portland, Oregon

32. **Untitled, c. 1993**
Sheet glass, stripped, kilnformed, and wheel cut
7½ x 6¼ x 6¼ inches (19 x 15.9 x 15.9 cm)
Anonymous lender, New York

33. **M/M/P-3, 1993 (#9)**
Collaboration with Dante Marioni
Sheet glass, kilnformed, picked up, blown incalmo, and etched
20¾ x 7½ inches max. diameter (52.7 x 19 cm)
Collection of Daniel Schwoerer and Lani McGregor, Portland, Oregon

34. **M/M/P-4, 1993 (#43)**
Collaboration with Dante Marioni
Sheet glass, kilnformed, picked up, blown incalmo, and etched
10¼ x 8⅛ inches diameter (26 x 20.6 cm)
Collection of Daniel Schwoerer and Lani McGregor, Portland, Oregon

35. **M/M/P-4, 1993 (#33)**
Collaboration with Dante Marioni
Sheet glass, kilnformed, picked up, blown incalmo, and etched
17¾ x 7¾ inches max. diameter (32.5 x 19.7 cm)
Collection of Brigitte Enders, Canberra, Australia

36. **Untitled 4, 1994 (#34)**
Sheet glass, stripped, kilnformed, and wheel cut
17¼ x 17¼ x 2½ inches (43.8 x 43.8 x 6.4 cm)
Collection of Daniel Greenberg and Susan Steinhauser, Los Angeles

37. **Untitled 1, 1984 (#2)**
Sheet glass, stripped, kilnformed, and wheel cut
13 x 12⅞ x 2⅛ inches (33 x 32.5 x 5.4 cm)
Collection of Dorothy and George Saxe, San Francisco

38. **Untitled, 1995**
Sheet glass, stripped, kilnformed, and wheel cut
13 x 10 x 3 inches (33 x 25.4 x 7.5 cm)
Collection of Arlene and Harold Schnitzer, Portland, Oregon

39. **Untitled, 1995 (#48)**
Sheet glass, stripped, kilnformed, and wheel cut
12⅝ x 8½ x 2¾ inches (32.2 x 21.6 x 7 cm)
Los Angeles County Museum of Art

40. **Untitled, 1995 (#6)**
Sheet glass, stripped, kilnformed, and wheel cut
2 x 20⅞ inches diameter (5 x 53 cm)
Collection of Daniel Schwoerer and Lani McGregor, Portland, Oregon

41. **Untitled, 1996**
Sheet glass, stripped, kilnformed, and wheel cut 95
11¾ x 11¾ x 2 inches (30 x 30 x 5 cm)
Private collection, New York

42. **Untitled 5, 1996**
Sheet glass, stripped, kilnformed, and wheel cut
11⅝ x 11⅝ x 1¾ inches (29.5 x 29.5 x 4.5 cm)
Courtesy of the artist and Bullseye Gallery, Portland, Oregon

43. **Untitled, 1997**
Sheet glass, stripped, kilnformed, and wheel cut
8¼ x 6¾ x 2 inches (20.3 x 15.2 x 5 cm)
Anonymous lender, New York

44. **Niijima 10, 1999-B 1**
Gaffer Scott Chaseling
Sheet glass, kilnformed, rolled up, and wheel cut
21¼ x 5¾ inches diameter (54 x 14.8 cm)
The Corning Museum of Glass; 14th Rakow Commission

45. **Niijima, 2000**
Gaffer: Scott Chaseling
Sheet glass, kilnformed, rolled up, and wheel cut
16 x 7¾ inches diameter (40.6 x 17.8 cm)
Private collection, New York

46. **Floating Red, 2000**
Sheet glass, fused and diamond polished
Four panels, each 28½ x 28½ inches (72.5 x 72.5 cm); set 58¼ x 58¼ inches (148 x 148 cm)
Courtesy of the artist and Bullseye Gallery, Portland, Oregon

47. **Untitled, 2000**
Sheet glass, stripped, kilnformed, and wheel cut
13¾ x 13¾ x 2½ inches (35 x 35 x 6.3 cm)
Anonymous lender, New York

48. **Untitled, 2003–05** (from the ***Impact Series***)
Sheet glass, stripped, kilnformed, and wheel cut
3 x 21 inches diameter (7.5 x 53.3 cm)
Private collection, New York

49. **Untitled, 2003–05** (from the ***Impact Series***)
Sheet glass, stripped, kilnformed, and wheel cut
3 x 21 inches diameter (7.5 x 53.3 cm)
Private collection, New York

50. **Untitled 4, 2005**
Sheet glass, fused and diamond polished
59 x 28¾ inches (150 x 73 cm)
Courtesy of the artist and Bullseye Gallery, Portland, Oregon

51. **Untitled 4, 2006** (from the ***Tumbling Lines Series***)
Sheet glass, stripped, kilnformed, and wheel cut
17½ x 17½ x 3 inches (44.2 x 44.2 x 7.5 cm)
Courtesy of the artist and Bullseye Gallery, Portland, Oregon

52. **Untitled 11, 2006**
Sheet glass, stripped, kilnformed, and wheel cut
17¾ x 17¾ x 2⅛ inches (45 x 45 x 5.5 cm)
Courtesy of the artist and Bullseye Gallery, Portland, Oregon

53. **Untitled 7, 2006**
Sheet glass, stripped, kilnformed, and wheel cut
17⅝ x 17⅝ x 2⅛ inches (44.7 x 44.7 x 5.5 cm)
Courtesy of the artist and Bullseye Gallery, Portland, Oregon

54. **Untitled 12, 2006** (from the ***Fragment Series***)
Sheet glass, stripped, kilnformed, and wheel cut
3 x 20⅞ inches diameter (7.5 x 53 x 53 cm)
Courtesy of the artist and Bullseye Gallery, Portland, Oregon

55. **Untitled 10, 2006**
Sheet glass, stripped, kilnformed, and wheel cut
3 x 21 inches diameter (7.5 x 53.5 cm)
Collection of David Kaplan and Glenn Ostergaard, Palm Springs, California

56. **Untitled 9, 2006**
Sheet glass, stripped, kilnformed, and wheel cut
18 x 18 x 3 inches (45.7 x 45.7 x 5.5 cm)
Courtesy of the artist and Bullseye Gallery, Portland, Oregon

57. **Untitled 9, 2006**
Sheet glass, stripped, kilnformed, and wheel cut
3 x 20⅞ inches diameter (7.5 x 53 cm)
Courtesy of the artist and Bullseye Gallery, Portland, Oregon

58. **Untitled 7, 2006**
Sheet glass, stripped, kilnformed, and wheel cut
11⅝ x 11⅝ x 2⅛ inches (29.5 x 29.5 x 5.5 cm)
Courtesy of the artist and Bullseye Gallery, Portland, Oregon

59. **Untitled 6, 2006**
Sheet glass, stripped, kilnformed, and wheel cut
3 x 21 inches diameter (7.5 x 53.3 cm)
Courtesy of the artist and Bullseye Gallery, Portland, Oregon

60. **Untitled 3, 2006**
Sheet glass, stripped, kilnformed, and wheel cut
3 x 20⅞ inches diameter (7.5 x 53 cm)
Courtesy of the artist and Bullseye Gallery, Portland, Oregon

61. **Untitled 5, 2006**
Sheet glass, stripped, kilnformed, and wheel cut
3 x 21 inches diameter (7.5 x 53.5 cm)
Courtesy of the artist and Bullseye Gallery, Portland, Oregon

62. **Untitled 11, 2006**
Sheet glass, stripped, kilnformed, and wheel cut
11¾ x 11¾ x 2⅛ (30 x 30 x 5.5 cm)
Courtesy of the artist and Bullseye Gallery, Portland, Oregon

63. **Untitled 2, 2006**
Sheet glass, fused and diamond polished
Nine panels: each 19 x 19 inches (48.3 x 48.3 cm); set 59 x 59 inches (150 x 150 cm)
Collection of Daniel Schwoerer and Lani McGregor, Portland, Oregon

64. **Untitled 10, 2006**
Sheet glass, fused and diamond polished
Eight panels: each 23 x 23 inches (58.5 x 58.5 cm); set 94½ x 47¼ inches (240 x 120 cm)
Courtesy of the artist and Bullseye Gallery, Portland, Oregon

65. **Untitled 2, 2006**
Sheet glass, fused and diamond polished
Four panels: each 31 x 31 inches (79 x 79 cm); set 63¾ x 63¾ inches (162 x 162 cm)
Courtesy of the artist and Bullseye Gallery, Portland, Oregon

66. **Untitled, 2007** (from the ***Rolling Lines Series***)
Gaffer Tom Rowney
Sheet glass, kilnformed, rolled up, and wheel cut
28 x 5 inches diameter (71 x 13 cm)
25 x 4 inches diameter (63.5 x 12 cm)
Courtesy of the artist and Bullseye Gallery, Portland, Oregon

67. **The Portland Panels: Choreographed Geometry, 2007**
Sheet glass, fused and diamond polished
Four panels: each 74½ x 47¼ inches (189.2 x 120 cm)
Courtesy of the artist and Bullseye Gallery, Portland, Oregon

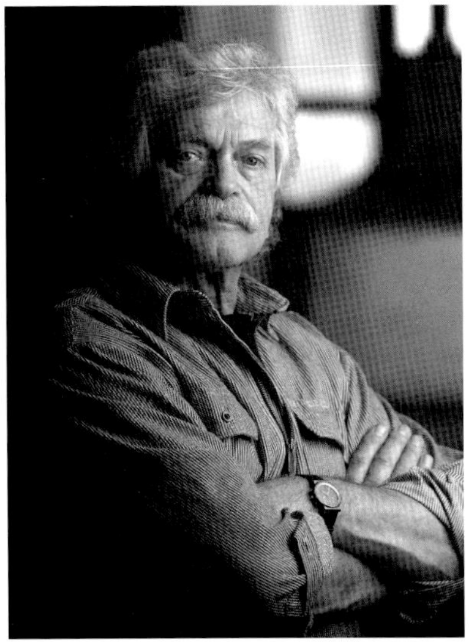

Klaus Moje

Born Hamburg, Germany, 1936
Resides Wapengo, New South Wales, Australia

Education/Training

1959 Master's certificate, Glass Schools Rheinbach and Hadamar
1955 Journeyman's certificate, training as glass cutter and grinder, Hamburg

Solo Exhibitions

2008 Cairns Regional Art Gallery, Queensland, Australia
2007 *Klaus Moje, New Work 2007*, Axia Modern Art, Melbourne
2006 *Klaus Moje: Glass—Living Treasures: Masters of Australian Craft*, Object Gallery, Sydney (touring exhibition)
2002 Axia Modern Art, Melbourne
2001 *The Klaus Moje Art Glass Exhibition*, Hsinchu Municipal Glass Museum, Taiwan (catalog)
2000 *SOFA/New York*, Bullseye Connection Gallery, New York
1998 Axia Modern Art, Melbourne
1997 *Klaus Moje—Recent Work*, Craft ACT Gallery, Canberra
1996 *Seattle Art Fair,* Ruth Summers Gallery
Klaus Moje—Glass, A Retrospective Exhibition, National Gallery of Victoria, Melbourne (1995–1996) (catalog)
Powerhouse Museum, Sydney
Canberra School of Art Gallery
Museum für Kunst und Gewerbe, Hamburg
American Craft Museum, New York
Wustum Museum of Fine Arts, Racine, Wisconsin
1994 Compositions Gallery, San Francisco
1993 *CINAF Chicago*, Habatat Galleries
1992 Gallery for Contemporary Art Niki, Tokyo
1991 *Dale Chihuly—Klaus Moje*, Glass Museum, Ebeltoft, Denmark
1989 Sanske Galerie, Zürich (repeatedly)
1987 Devise Gallery, Melbourne
1987 Habatat Galleries, Miami/Boca Raton, Florida
1985 *John Kuhn—Klaus Moje—Richard Ritter at the Glass Art Gallery*, Toronto
Kurland/Summers Gallery, Los Angeles (repeatedly)
Glass Artists Gallery, Sydney
1982 Galerie SM, Frankfurt
1981 Foster/White Gallery, Seattle
Habatat Galleries, Detroit (repeatedly)
Heller Gallery, New York (repeatedly)
Galerie Lietzow, Berlin
1980 Retrospective, Museum für Kunst und Gewerbe, Hamburg
1979 Contemporary Art Glass Gallery, New York
1973 The British Crafts Centre, London

Selected Collections

The Art Gallery of Western Australia, Perth
Auckland Museum, New Zealand
Australian National Gallery, Canberra
Australian National University Collection, Canberra
Badisches Landesmuseum, Karlsruhe, Germany
Bayerischer Kunstgewerbe-Verein, Munich
Canberra City Art Museum
Carnegie-Mellon University, Pittsburgh
Chrysler Museum of Art, Norfolk, Virginia
Cincinnati Art Museum
Cooper-Hewitt Museum, New York
Corning Museum of Glass, Corning, New York
Detroit Institute of Art
Fine Arts Museum of San Francisco
Ernsting Stiftung, Alter Hof, Herding, Germany
Geelong Art Gallery, Australia
Gemeentemuseum Den Hague, The Hague
Glasmuseum Frauenau, Germany
Grassi Museum, Leipzig, Germany
Hamilton Art Gallery, Australia
Hsinchu Cultural Center, Taiwan
Kestnermuseum, Hanover, Germany
Kunstgewerbemuseum Darmstadt, Germany
Kunstgewerbemuseum, Berlin
Kunstgewerbemuseum, Cologne
Kunstgewerbemuseum, Prague
Kunstmuseum Düsseldorf, Germany
Kulturgeschichliches Museeum, Osnabrück, Germany
Kunstsammlungen der Veste, Coburg, Germany
La Trobe University Collection, Melbourne
Landesmuseum Oldenburg, Germany
Landesmuseum Schleswig-Holstein, Schleswig, Germany
Lobmeyr Museum, Vienna
Los Angeles County Museum of Art
Metropolitan Museum of Art, New York
Minneapolis Institute of Arts, Minnesota
Mint Museum of Craft + Design, Charlotte, North Carolina
Montreal Museum of Fine Arts, Toronto
Musée de Design d'Arts Appliqués Contemporains, Lausanne, Switzerland
Museum Bellerive, Zürich
Museum für Kunst und Gewerbe, Hamburg
Museum of Arts and Design, New York (formerly American Craft Museum)
Museum of Modern Art, Hokkaido, Japan
National Gallery of Victoria, Melbourne
National Museums of Scotland, Edinburgh
Novy Bor Museum, Novy Bor, Czech Republic
Palm Springs Art Museum, California
Powerhouse Museum, Sydney
Queensland Art Gallery, Brisbane, Australia
Racine Art Museum, Wisconsin
Glasmuseet, Ebeltoft, Denmark
Schloss Cappenberg, Dortmund, Germany
Seattle Art Museum, Washington
Shimonoseki City Art Museum, Japan
Speed Art Museum, Louisville, Kentucky
Städtisches Museum, Göttingen, Germany
Toledo Museum of Art, Ohio
Toyama Glass Museum, Japan
University of Wisconsin Art Collection, Madison
Victoria and Albert Museum, London
Wagga Wagga City Art Gallery, Australia
Württembergisches Landesmuseum, Stuttgart

Awards, Honors, and Grants

2008	Lifetime Membership Award, Ausglass, Canberra
2006	Honorary Officer (AO), General Division of the Order of Australia
2005	Australia Council Fellowship
2004	Lifetime Achievement Award, UrbanGlass, Brooklyn
2000	Lifetime Achievement Award, Glass Art Society, New York
1999	Bavarian State Award, Munich
	Rakow Commission, Corning Museum of Glass, Corning, New York
1997	UrbanGlass Award for Innovation in a Glassworking Technique, Brooklyn
1996	Honorary Life Membership, "Arbeitsgemeinschaft des Kunsthandwerks," Hamburg
1985	Dr. Maedebach Memorial Prize, "Preis für Moderne Glasgestaltung in Europa," Coburger Glass, Germany
1984	Suntory Museum Prize, *Glass '84 In Japan*, Tokyo/Kobe
1976	Bavarian State Award, Gold Medal, joint with Isgard Moje-Wohlgemuth, Munich (1969–76)
1971	Hessen State Award for German Decorative Art, Germany
1956	First Prize, Competition of German Journeymen, Germany